The Evolution of Fashion

by Florence Mary Gardiner

PREFACE.

In compiling this volume on Costume (portions of which originally appeared in the Ludgate Illustrated Magazine, under the editorship of Mr. A. J. Bowden), I desire to acknowledge the valuable assistance I have received from sources not usually available to the public; also my indebtedness to the following authors, from whose works I have quoted:--Mr. Beck, Mr. R. Davey, Mr. E. Rimmel, Mr. Knight, and the late Mr. J. R. Planch? I also take this opportunity of thanking Messrs. Liberty and Co., Messrs. Jay, Messrs. E. R. Garrould, Messrs. Walery, Mr. Box, and others, who have offered me special facilities for consulting drawings, engravings, &c., in their possession, many of which they have courteously allowed me to reproduce, by the aid of Miss Juliet Hensman, and other artists.

The book lays no claim to being a technical treatise on a subject which is practically inexhaustible, but has been written with the intention of bringing before the general public in a popular manner circumstances which have influenced in a marked degree the wearing apparel of the British Nation.

FLORENCE MARY GARDINER.

West Kensington, 1897.

CONTENTS.

CHAPTER.

THE EVOLUTION OF FASHION

CHAPTER I.

THE DRESS, B.C. 594--A.D. 1897.

"Fashions that are now called new Have been worn by more than you; Elder times have used the same, Though these new ones get the name."

Middleton's "Mayor of Quinborough."

A hard fate has condemned human beings to enter this mortal sphere without any natural covering, like that possessed by the lower animals to protect them from the extremes of heat and cold. Had this been otherwise, countless myriads, for untold ages, would have escaped the tyrannical sway of the goddess Fashion, and the French proverb, il faut souffrir pour 陰 re belle, need never have been written.

The costume of our progenitors was chiefly remarkable for its extreme simplicity; and, as far as we can gather, no difference in design was made between the sexes. A few leaves entwined by the stalks, the feathers of birds, the bark of trees, or roughly-dressed skins of animals were probably regarded by beaux and belles of the Adamite period as beautiful and appropriate adornments for the body, and were followed by garments made from plaited grass, which was doubtless the origin of weaving, a process which is nothing more than the mechanical plaiting of hair, wool, flax, &c. In many remote districts these primitive fashions still prevail, as, for example, in Madras, where, at an annual religious ceremony, it is customary for the low caste natives to exchange for a short period their usual attire for an apron of leaves. In the Brazilian forests the lecythis, or "shirt tree," is to be found, from which the people roll off the bark in short lengths, and, after making it pliable in water, cut two slits for the arm-holes and one for the neck, when their dress is complete and ready for use. The North American Indian employs feathers for purposes of the toilet, and many African tribes are noted for their deftly-woven fabrics composed of grass and other vegetable fibres, while furs and skins are essential articles of dress in Northern latitudes. Perhaps the earliest specimen of a modiste's bill in existence has recently been found on a chalk tablet at Nippur, in Chaldea. The hieroglyphics record ninety-two robes and tunics: fourteen of these were perfumed with myrrh, aloes and cassia. The date of this curious antique cannot be less than two thousand eight hundred years before the Christian era. In ancient times it must be remembered that the principal seats of civilisation were Assyria and Egypt, and upon these countries Western nations depended for many of the luxuries of life. The Jews derived their fine fabrics from the latter place, which was particularly noted for its linen manufactures and for magnificent embroideries, of which the accompanying illustration will give some idea. Medes and Babylonians, of the highest class, partially arrayed themselves in silk, which cost its weight in gold, and about the time of Ezekiel (B.C. 594) it is known to have been used in the dress of the Persians. It is a remarkable circumstance that this animal product was brought to the West manufactured in cloth, which was only half silk; and it is said the plan was devised of unravelling the stuff, which was rewoven into cloth of entire silk. Owing to its high price, the Romans forbade its being used for the entire dress by men, complete robes of silk being reserved for women. It is numbered among the extravagant luxuries of Heliogabalus that he was the first man who wore a silken garment, and the anecdote is well known of the Emperor Aurelian, who refused, on the ground of its extravagant cost, a silk dress which his consort earnestly desired to possess.

Monuments still in existence show that the Egyptians, owing to the warmth of their climate, were partial to garments of a semi-transparent character, while those living on the banks of the Tigris, who were subjected to greater extremes of temperature, wore clothing of similar design, but of wool, with heavy fringes of the same as a trimming. In some cases this feature of Assyrian costume is shown in double rows, one pendent, while the other stands out in a horizontal direction.

The early Greek dress, or chiton, was a very simple contrivance, reaching to the feet. If ungirdled, it would trail on the ground; but generally it was drawn through the zone or waistbelt in such a manner that it was double to the extent of about thirty inches over the vital organs of the body. The great distinction between male and female dress consisted in the length of the skirt. The trimmings were of embroidery, woven diapers, figure bands with chariots and horses; and, in some cases, glass ornaments and thin metal plates were applied. Among the working classes the chiton was, of course, homespun, or of leather.

The stola was the Roman equivalent for the nineteenth century robe or gown, and in many respects resembled the Greek chiton. The fabrics employed were wool and linen up to the end of the Republic, though at a later date, as has already been stated, silk was imported. Colour, under the Emperors, was largely used, and at least thirteen shades of the dye obtained from the murex, which passed under the general name of purple, could be seen in the costume of both sexes.

When the Roman Empire was dismembered (A.D. 395) a style of dress seems to have flourished in the important towns of the Mediterranean, which was similar to that worn in medi 鋬 al times in Britain, and which may be examined in the specimens of statuary adorning tombs of the twelfth and thirteenth centuries. The semi-tight under-dress and sleeves appear to have been elaborately embroidered, and the loose mantle of plain material was edged with a border.

One of the earliest descriptions of the female dress in Britain is that of Boadicea, the Queen of the Iceni, whom we are told wore a tunic woven chequerwise in purple, red, and blue. Over this was a shorter garment open on the bosom, and leaving the arms bare. Her yellow hair flowed over her shoulders, upon which rested an ample cloak, secured by a fibula (brooch). A torque, or necklet, was also worn; a pair of bronze breastplates as a protection from the Roman arrows, and her fingers and arms were covered with rings and bracelets.

The costume of the Anglo-Saxon ladies consisted of a sherte, or camise, of linen next the skin, a kirtle, which resembled the modern petticoat, and a gunna, or gown, with sleeves. Out of doors a mantle covered the upper portion of the body, and with the coverchief, or head rail, formed a characteristic feature of the dress of the day. Cloth, silk, and linen were the favourite materials for clothing, and red, blue, yellow, and green the fashionable colours. Very little black and white were used at this period. Saxon women were renowned for their skill with the needle, and used large quantities of gold thread and jewels in their work. Among other instances quoted, Queen Editha embroidered the coronation mantle of her husband, Edward the Confessor.

For some years after the Norman Conquest, women retained the costume of the Anglo-Saxon period, with certain additions and modifications. Fine coloured cloths and richest furs were used by both sexes, and sleeves and trains were such a length that it was found necessary to knot them, so that they should not trail upon the ground.

The next important change was the surcoat and tight bodice, which was fastened in front to fit the figure.

There are evident traces that as civilisation advanced the love of dress and the desire of the fair sex to appear beautiful in the eyes of all beholders increased in like proportion. From ancient MSS. and other sources, we have ample proof of this. St. Jerome calls women "philoscomon," that is to say, lovers of finery, and another writer states: "One of the most difficult points to manage with women is to root out their curiosity for clothes and ornaments for the body." St. Bernard admonished his sister with greater candour than politeness on her visiting him, well arraied with riche clothinge, with perles and precious stones: "Such pompe and pride to adorne a carion as is youre body. Thinke ye not of the pore people, that be deyen for hunger and colde; and that for the sixth parte of youre gay arraye, forty persons might be clothed, refreshed, and kepte from the colde?"

The increased facilities for travelling offered to those engaged in the Crusades, and the necessary intercourse with other nations, caused considerable quantities of foreign materials to be imported to England during the Middle Ages: and this had a corresponding effect upon the costume of the period, which was chiefly remarkable for its richness and eccentricity of form. Among the materials in use may be mentioned diaper cloth from Ypres, a town in Flanders, famous for its rich dress stuffs; tartan, called by the French "tyretaine," meaning teint, or colour of Tyre (scarlet being indifferently used for purple by ancient writers, and including all the gradations of colour formed by a mixture of blue and red, from indigo to crimson). There was a fine white woollen cloth called Blanket, named after its inventor, Sarcenet, also from its Saracenic origin, and gauze which was made at Gaza in Palestine. Ermine was strictly confined to the use of the Royal Family and nobles, and cloth of gold, and habits embroidered with jewellery, or lined with minever or other expensive fur, could only be worn by knights and ladies with incomes exceeding 400 marks per annum. Those who had not more than 200 marks were permitted to wear silver cloth, with ribands, girdles, &c., reasonably embellished; also woollen cloth not costing more than six marks the piece.

The tight forms of dress now in common use among women were an incentive to tight lacing, an injurious practice, from which their descendants suffer. A lady is described

"Clad in purple pall, With gentyll body and middle small,"

and another damsel, whose splendid girdle of beaten gold was embellished with emeralds and rubies, evidently, from the description, had a waist which was not the size intended by Nature.

During the Wars of the Roses both trade and costume made little progress, and after the union of the Houses of York and Lancaster by the marriage of Henry VII. with his Queen, Elizabeth, their attention was chiefly concerned in filling their impoverished coffers, which left them little opportunity for promoting new fashions in dress. Henry VIII. afforded ample facilities for the revival of the trade in dress goods, and there is little difficulty in tracing female costume of the sixteenth century when we remember that in the course of thirty-eight years he married six wives, besides having them painted times without number by all the popular artists of the day.

J. R. Planch?in his "History of British Costume," says: "The gowns of the nobility were magnificent, and at this period were open in front to the waist, showing the kirtle, or inner garment, as what we should call the petticoat was then termed." Anne of Cleves, who found so little favour in Henry's eyes, is said to have worn at their first interview "a rich gowne of cloth of gold made round, without any train, after the Dutch fashion;" and in a wardrobe account of the eighth year of this Bluebeard's reign appears the following item: "Seven yards of purple cloth of damask gold for a kirtle for Queen Catherine of Arragon." The dress of Catherine Parr is thus described by Pedro de Gante, secretary to the Spanish Duke de Najera, who visited Henry VIII. in 1543-1544: "She was robed in cloth of gold, with a 'saya' (petticoat) of brocade, the sleeves lined with crimson satin and trimmed with three-piled crimson velvet. Her train was more than two yards long." Articles of dress were often bequeathed by will. In one made on the 14th of August, 1540, William Cherington, yeoman, of Waterbeche, leaves "To my mother my holyday gowne." Nicholas, Dyer of Feversham, 29th October, 1540, "To my sister, Alice Bichendyke, thirteen shillings and ninepence which she owed me, and two kerchiefs of holland." John Holder, rector of Gamlingay, in 1544 leaves to Jane Greene "my clothe frock lined with satin cypress." These entries are from wills in the Ely Registry.

A peculiar feature in the costume of both sexes was sleeves distinct from the gown, but attached (so as to be changed at pleasure) to the waistcoat. Among the inventories we find three pairs of purple satin sleeves for women, one pair of linen sleeves paned with gold over the arm, quilted with black silk and wrought with flowers; one pair of sleeves of purple gold tissue damask wire, each one tied with aglets of gold; one pair of crimson satin sleeves, four buttons of gold being set on each, and in every button nine pearls.

We are all familiar with the distended skirts, jewelled stomachers and enormous ruffs which adorned the virgin form of Good Queen Bess. In the middle of her reign the body was imprisoned in whalebone, and the fardingale, the prototype of the modern hoop, was introduced, as it was not to be supposed that a lady who is said to have left three thousand dresses in her wardrobe would remain faithful to the fashions of her grandmother; and Elizabeth's love of dress permeated all classes of society.

The portrait of Mary Queen of Scots, who was considered an authority on matters of the toilet, and whose taste for elegance of apparel had been cultivated to a high degree during her residence at the French Court is given. There is a subtlety and charm about it which is wanting in the costume of her cousin Elizabeth, and it may be considered a fair type of what was worn by a gentlewoman of that period. The full skirt appears to fall in easy folds, and the basqued bodice, with tight sleeves, is closely moulded to the figure and surmounted by an elaborately-constructed ruff of muslin and lace.

To the great regret of antiquarians, the wardrobes of our ancient kings, formerly kept at the Tower, were by the order of James I. distributed. At no period was the costume of Britain more picturesque than in the middle of the seventeenth century, and we naturally turn to its great delineators Velasquez, Van Dyck, Rembrandt, and Rubens, who delighted in giving us such fine examples of their work. Women had grown tired of the unwieldy fardingale, and changed it for graceful gowns with flowing skirts and low bodices, finished with deep vandyked collars of lace or embroidery.

A studied negligence, an elegance prevailed in the Stuart Court, particularly after the Restoration. Charles II.'s bevy of beauties are similarly attired, and the pictures in Hampton Court show us women whose snowy necks and arms are no longer veiled, and whose gowns of rich satin, with voluminous trains, are piled up in the background. Engravings and drawings which may be seen in every printseller's window make special illustrations of this period unnecessary.

Dutch fashions appear to have followed in the wake of William and Mary. Stomachers and tight sleeves were once more in favour, and fabrics of a rich and substantial character were employed in preference to the softer makes of silk, which lent itself so well to the soft flowing lines of the previous era.

An intelligent writer has remarked "that Fashion from the time of George I. has been such a varying goddess that neither history, tradition, nor painting has been able to preserve all her mimic forms; like Proteus struggling in the arms of Telemachus, on the Phanaic coast, she passed from shape to shape with the rapidity of thought." In 1745 the hoop had increased at the sides and diminished in front, and a pamphlet was published in that year entitled "The enormous abomination of the hoop petticoat, as the fashion now is." Ten years later it is scarcely discernible in some figures, and in 1757 reappears, extending right and left after the manner of the court dress of the reign of George III. For the abolition of this monstrosity we are indebted to George IV., and ladies' dresses then rushed to the other extreme. Steel and whalebone was dispensed with, and narrow draperies displayed the form they were supposed to conceal, and were girdled just below the shoulders.

These were in time followed by the bell-shaped skirts worn at the accession of Her Majesty Queen Victoria, during whose reign fashion has indeed run riot. The invention of the sewing machine was the signal for the appearance of frills and furbelows, and meretricious ornament of every kind. In the middle of the present century crinolines were again to the fore, skirts were proportionately wide and generally flounced to the top. The bodice terminated at the waist with a belt; but in some cases a Garibaldi, or loose bodice of different texture, was substituted. The next change to be noted was that hideous garment the "polonaise," which was a revival of, and constructed on similar lines to, the "super froc" of the Middle Ages. For many years English ladies, with a supreme disregard for the appropriate, wore this with a skirt belonging to an entirely different costume. But at last people got nauseated with these abominations, and under the gentle sway and influence of "Our Princess" a prettier, more useful and rational costume appeared. In

1876 the graceful Princess dress, which accentuated every good point in the figure, was generally worn; and though this costume in the latter part of its career was fiercely abused by the rotund matron and Mrs. Grundy, for clinging too closely to the lines of the human form, it was distinctly an advance as regards health and beauty on the varying styles which preceded it.

The aesthetic movement has also had a marked influence on our taste in all directions, but more especially in the costume of the last few years; and though the picturesque garb of the worshippers of the sunflower and the lily may not be adapted to the wear and tear of this workaday world, it is beautiful in form and design, incapable of undue pressure; and for children and young girls it would be difficult to imagine a more charming, artistic, and becoming costume.

Once more we are eschewing classical lines for grotesque which makes caricatures of lovely women, and drives plain ones to despair. The subdued and delicate tints which a few seasons since were regarded with favour have been superseded by garish shades and bright colours, which seem to quarrel with everything in Nature and Art. Unfortunately, we English are prone to extremes, and possess the imitative rather than the creative faculty. Consequently, our national costume is seldom distinctive, but a combination of some of the worst styles of our Continental neighbours, who would scorn to garb themselves with so little regard for fitness, beauty, and the canons of good taste.

Two dominant notes, however, have been struck in the harmonies of costume during the last twenty-five years--the tailor-made dress, which may almost be regarded as a national livery; and the tea gown, that reposeful garment to which we affectionately turn in our hours of ease. How well each in its way is calculated to serve the purpose for which it is designed, the simple cloth, tweed, or serge costume moulded to the lines of the figure, adapted to our changeful climate, and giving a cachet to the wearer, not always found in much more costly apparel, a rational costume in the best sense of the word, and one which women of all ages may assume with satisfaction to themselves and to those with whom they come in contact. The tea gown, on the other hand, drapes the figure loosely so as to fall in graceful folds, and may be regarded as a distinct economy, as it so often takes the place of a more expensive dress. Beauty, which is one of Heaven's best gifts to women, is useless unless appropriately framed, and a well-known exponent on the art of dressing artistically, has laid down the axiom that harmonies of colour are more successful than contrasts. If we turn to Nature we have an unfailing source of inspiration. The foliage tints, sunset effects, the animal and mineral worlds all offer schemes of colour, which can be readily adapted to our persons and surroundings. And to look our best and, above all, to grow old gracefully, is a duty which every daughter of Eve owes to humanity. The manner in which so many women give way early in life is simply appalling. While still in the bloom of womanhood they assume the habits and dress of decrepitude, submit to be placed on the social shelf without a murmur, and calmly allow those slightly their junior, and in some cases their senior, to appropriate the good things of life, and to monopolise the attention of all and sundry. Mothers in their prime willingly allow anyone who can be persuaded to do so, to chaperone their daughters, and to pilot them through the social eddies and quicksands of their first season, and through sheer indolence fail to exercise the lawful authority and responsibility which maternity entails. The unmarried woman, conscious that she is no longer in her first youth, and indifferent to the charms of maturity, takes to knitting socks in obscure corners, and assumes an air of self-repression and middle-agedness which apparently takes ten years from her span of existence, and conveys to the casual onlooker, that she has passed the boundary line between youth and old age. Why should these women sink before their time into a slough of dowdyism and cut themselves off from the enjoyments civilisation has provided for their benefit?

Equally to be deprecated are those who cling so desperately to youth that they entirely forget the later stages of life have their compensations. Women who in crowded ballrooms display their redundant or attenuated forms to the gaze of all beholders, whose coiffure owes more to art than nature, and who comfort themselves with the conviction that in a carefully shaded light rouge and pearl powder are hardly distinguishable from the bloom of a youthful and healthy complexion. A variety of circumstances combine to bring into the world a race of people who cannot strictly lay claim to beauty, but who nevertheless have many good points which might be accentuated, while those that are less pleasing could be concealed. A middleaged woman will respect herself and be more respected by others if she drapes her person in velvet, brocade, and other rich fabrics which fall in stately folds, and give her dignity, than if she persists in decking herself in muslin, crepon, net, and similar materials, because in the long since past they suited her particular style. Gossamers belong to the young, with their dimpled arms, shoulders of snowy whiteness, and necks like columns of ivory. Their eyes are brighter than jewels, and their luxuriant locks need no ornament save a rose nestling in its green leaves, a fit emblem of youth and beauty.

With the education and art training at present within the grasp of all classes of the community there is nothing to prevent our modifying prevailing fashions to our own requirements; and common sense ought to teach us (even if we ignore every other sentiment which is supposed to guide reasoning creatures) that one particular style cannot be appropriate to women who are exact opposites to each other. If each person would only think out for herself raiment beautiful in form, rich in texture, and adapted to the daily needs of life, we should be spared a large number of the startling incongruities which offend the eye in various directions.

CHAPTER II.

CURIOUS HEADGEAR.

"Here in her hair The painter plays the spider, and hath woven A golden mesh to entrap the hearts of men Faster than gnats in cobwebs."

The Merchant of Venice.

Holy Writ simply teems with allusions to the luxurious tresses of the fair daughters of the East, and there is little doubt that at an early period in the world's history women awakened to the fact that a well-tired head was a very potent attraction, and had a recognised market value. Jewish women were particularly famed in this respect, and employed female barbers, who, with the aid of crisping pins, horns, and towers, prepared their clients for conquest. These jewelled horns were generally made of the precious metals, and the position denoted the condition of the wearer. A married woman had it fixed on the right side of the head, a widow on the left, and she who was still an unappropriated blessing on the crown. Over the horn the veil was thrown coquettishly, as in the illustration. Assyrian women delighted in long ringlets, confined by a band of metal, and the men were not above the weakness of plaiting gold wire with their beards. Rimmel, in "The Book of Perfumes," relates a curious anecdote of Mausolus, King of Caria, who turned his people's fondness for flowing locks to account when his exchequer required replenishing. "Having first had a quantity of wigs made and stored in the royal warehouses, he published an edict compelling all his subjects to have their heads shaved. A few days after, the monarch's agents went round, offering them the perukes destined to cover their denuded polls, which they were delighted to buy at any price". It is not surprising that Artemisia could not console herself for the loss of such a clever husband, and that, not satisfied with drinking his ashes dissolved in wine, she spent some of her lamented lord's ill-gotten revenue in building such a monument to his memory that it was counted one of the wonders of the world.

The Egyptians were also partial to wigs, some of which are still preserved in the British Museum. Ladies wore a multitude of small plaits and jewelled head-pieces resembling peacocks and other animals, which contrasted with their dark tresses with brilliant effect; or a fillet ornamented with a lotus bud. The coiffure of a princess was remarkable for its size and the abundance of animal, vegetable, and mineral treasures with which it was adorned. In Egyptian tombs and elsewhere have been discovered small wooden combs resembling the modern tooth-comb, and metal mirrors of precisely the same shape as those in use at the present day, as well as numerous other toilet appliances.

Grecian sculpture affords us the opportunity of studying the different modes in favour in that country, and it is astonishing to find what a variety of methods were adopted by the belles of ancient Greece for enhancing their charms. A loose knot, fastened by a clasp in the form of a grasshopper, was a favourite fashion. Cauls of network, metal mitres of different designs, and simple bands, and sometimes chaplets, of flowers, all confined at different periods, the luxuriant locks of the Helens, Penelopes, and Xantippes of ancient times.

It was a common custom among heathen nations to consecrate to their gods the hair when cut off, as well as that growing on the head, and it was either consumed on the altar, deposited in temples, or hung upon the trees. A famous instance of the consecration of hair is that of Berenice, the wife of Ptolemy Evergetes. It is related that when the king went on his expedition to Syria, she, solicitous for his safety, made a vow to consecrate her hair (which was remarkable for its fineness and beauty) to Venus, if he returned to her. When her husband came back she kept her word, and offered her hair in the temple of Cyprus. This was afterwards missing, when a report was spread that it had been turned into a constellation in the heavens, which constellation, an old writer tells us, is called Coma Berenices (the hair of Berenice) to the present day. Another remarkable instance is that of Nero, who, according to Suetonius, cut off his first beard, put it in a casket of gold set with jewels, and consecrated it to Jupiter Capitolinus.

The hair of the head and beard appears to have been held in great respect by most nations, and perhaps we may trace the use of human hair in spells and incantations to this fact. Orientals especially treat the hair which falls from them with superstitious care, and bury it, so that no one shall use it to their prejudice.

Roman matrons generally preferred blonde hair to their own ebon tresses, and resorted to wigs and dye when Nature, as they considered, had treated them unkindly. Ovid rebukes a lady of his acquaintance in the plainest terms for having destroyed her hair.

"Did I not tell you to leave off dyeing your hair? Now you have no hair left to dye: and yet nothing was handsomer than your locks: they came down to your knees, and were so fine that you were afraid to comb them. Your own hand has been the cause of the loss you deplore: you poured the poison on your own head. Now Germany will send you slaves' hair--a vanquished nation will supply your ornament. How many times, when you hear people praising the beauty of your hair, you will blush and say to yourself: 'It is bought ornament to which I owe my beauty, and I know not what Sicambrian virgin they are admiring in me. And yet there was a time when I deserved all these compliments.'"

It would puzzle any fin de sile husband or brother to express his displeasure in more appropriate words than those chosen by the poet.

The Britons, before they mixed with other nations, were a fair-haired race, and early writers referred to their washing their auburn tresses in water boiled with lime to increase the reddish colour. Boadicea is described with flowing locks which fell upon her shoulders; but after the Roman Invasion the hair of both men and women followed the fashion of the conquerors.

From Planch?s "History of British Costume," we learn that "the female head-dress among all classes of the Anglo-Saxons was a long piece of linen or silk wrapped round the head and neck." It appears to have been called a head-rail, or wimple, but was dispensed with in the house, as the hair was then as cherished an ornament as at the present day. A wife described by Adhelm, Bishop of Sherborne, who wrote in the eighth century, is said to have had "twisted locks, delicately curled by the iron;" and in the poem of "Judith" the heroine is called "the maid of the Creator, with twisted locks." Two long plaits were worn by Norman ladies, and were probably adopted by our own countrywomen after the Conquest.

During the Middle Ages feminine head-gear underwent many changes.

Golden nets, and linen bands closely pinned round the hair and chin, were followed by steeple-shaped erections and horned head-dresses in a variety of shapes, of which the accompanying sketches will give a better idea than any written description.

During the sixteenth century matrons adopted either a pointed hood, composed of velvet or other rich fabric, often edged with fur, a close-fitting coif, or the French cap to be seen in the portraits of the unhappy Mary Stuart. Those who were unmarried had their hair simply braided and embellished with knots of ribbon, strings of pearls, or Nature's most beautiful adornment for the maiden--sweet-scented flowers.

The auburn tresses of Her Gracious Majesty Queen Elizabeth, were always bien coiff 閑, if we may judge from her various portraits. She scorned the hoods, lace caps, and pointed coifs, worn by her contemporaries, and adopted a miniature crown or jaunty hat of velvet, elaborately jewelled. Her fair complexion and light hair were thrown into relief by ruffles of lace, and this delicate fabric was stretched over fine wire frames, which met at the back, and remotely suggested the fragile wings of the butterfly, or the nimbus of a saint, neither of which ornaments was particularly appropriate to the lady in question. The front hair was turned over a cushion, or dressed in stiff sausage-like curls, pinned close to the head, and was adorned with strings and stars of flashing gems and a pendant resting on the forehead.

That splendid historian, Stubbs, who has left us such minute particulars of the fashions of his time, quaintly describes the coiffure of the ladies of the Court. He states: "It must be curled, frizzled, crisped, laid out in wreaths and borders from one ear to the other, and lest it should fall down, must be underpropped with forkes and weirs, and ornamented with gold or silver curiously wrought. Such gewgaws, which being unskilful in woman's tearms, I cannot easily recount. Then upon the toppes of their stately turrets, stand their other capital ornaments: a French hood, hatte, cappe, kircher and suchlike, whereof some be of velvet, some of this fashion and some of that. Cauls made of netwire, that the cloth of gold, silver, or tinsel, with which their hair was sometimes covered, might be seen through; and lattice caps with three horns or corners, like the forked caps of popish priests." The Harleian MSS., No. 1776, written in the middle of Elizabeth's reign, refers to an ordinance for the reformation of gentlewomen's head-dress, and says: "None shall wear an ermine or lattice bonnet unless she be a gentlewoman born, having Arms." This latter phrase, we may conclude, refers to armorial bearings, not to physical development.

The wearing of false hair and periwigs was left to the sterner sex for some years after the restoration of the House of Stuart, and women were satisfied with well-brushed ringlets escaping from a bandeau of pearls, or beautified by a single flower. The hair was often arranged in small, flat curls on the forehead, as in the sketch of a Beauty of the Court of Charles II.; and this fashion had a softening effect on the face, and was known as the "Sevign?style."

Dutch fashions naturally prevailed in the Court of William and Mary, and this queen is represented with a high muslin cap, adorned with a series of upright frills, edged with lace, and long lappets falling on the shoulders. Farquhar, in his comedy "Love and the Bottle," alludes to the "high top-knots," and Swift, to the "pinners edged with colberteen," as the lace streamers were called. About this period the hair was once again rolled back from the face, and assumed enormous dimensions, so much so, that in some cases it was found necessary to make doorways broader and higher than they had hitherto been, to allow fashionably-dressed ladies to pass through without displacing the elaborate erections they carried. Stuffed with horsehair, clotted with pomade and powder, and decked with every conceivable ornament, from a miniature man-of-war in full sail, to a cooing dove with outspread wings, presumably sitting on its nest, or a basket of flowers wreathed with ribbons. Naturally, the aid of the barber was called in, as ladies were incapable of constructing and manipulating such a mass of tangled locks. We may imagine, on the score of expense and for other reasons, the hair was not dressed so frequently as cleanliness demanded, for in a book on costume a hairdresser is described as asking one of his customers how long it was since her hair had been opened and repaired. On her replying, "Nine weeks," he mildly suggested that that was as long as a head could well go in summer, "and, therefore, it was proper to deliver it now, as it began to be a little hazarde." Various anecdotes of this nature make us feel that personal hygiene was a matter of secondary importance to our ancestors.

Planch? in his work on British Costume, informs us that powder maintained its ground till 1793, when it was discarded by Her Majesty Queen Charlotte, Consort of George III., and the Princesses.

Varied, indeed, have been the fashions of the 19th century, the close of which is fast approaching. Only a few of the styles adopted can be briefly touched upon, and, naturally, those will be selected which form the greatest contrast to each other. The belle of 1830 was distinguished by upstanding bows of plain or plaited hair, arranged on the crown of the head, and the front was generally in bands or short ringlets, held in place by tortoise-shell side-combs. The simplicity of this coiffure was compensated for by the enormous size of the hats and bonnets generally worn with it. These had wide and curiously-shaped brims, over which was stretched or gathered silk, satin, aerophane, or similar materials. Garlands and bunches of flowers and feathers were used in profusion, and bows and strings of gauze ribbon floated in the wind. In this bewitching costume were our grandmothers wooed and won by suitors who evidently, from the impassioned love letters still in existence, believed them to be perfect types of loveliness.

Towards the middle of Queen Victoria's reign, the hair was dressed in a simple knot, and the front arranged in ringlets, which fell gracefully on the chest and shoulders. Even youthful married ladies, in the privacy of their homes and for morning dress, were expected, by one of those potent but unwritten laws of the fickle goddess Fashion, to wear muslin or net caps, with lace borders, embellished with ribbons.

The labours of Hercules would be mere child's play compared to giving a faithful record of the chameleon-like changes which have affected that kaleidoscope, public taste, during the last forty years, and a very limited study of this fascinating subject at once convinces us that, whatever peculiarities may appear, they are certain to be revivals or modifications of styles favoured by our more or less remote ancestors.

In 1872 loomed upon us that ghastly horror the chignon, which bore a faint resemblance to the exaggerated coiffures of the 18th century. Upon this monstrous edifice, with its seductive Alexandra curl, were tilted bonnets so minute that they were almost invisible in the mountains of hair that surrounded them. These were replaced by hats ?la Chinois, like shallow plates; while for winter wear, others of fur or feathers were introduced, with an animal's head fixed firmly on the brow of the wearer, and resembling nothing so much as the fox foot-warmer, with which ladies now keep their pedal extremities at a proper temperature when enjoying an airing. Besides these, there were pinched canoes turned keel uppermost, and flexible mushrooms, which flapped and caught the wind till it was necessary to attach a string to the edge, to keep them snug and taut; such hats as Leech has immortalised in his sketches. Turbans and facsimiles of the delicious but indigestible pork-pie, Gainsborough, Rousby, and Langtry hats, all named after styles worn by their respective namesakes; and hats made of straw, leghorn, crinoline, lace, satin, and of silver and gold tissue, of every shape and size that fancy could devise, or the heart of the most exacting woman of fashion could desire. The hair beneath was dressed like the frizzy mop illustrated, in plaited wedges flowing like a pendant hump half-way down the back, or in a cascade of curls reaching from the crown of the head to the waist. These were followed by gigantic rolls at the back of the skull, Grecian knots, varying from the dimensions of a door handle to those of a cottage loaf, and latterly by that hideous monstrosity, the "bun." Another turn of the wheel of fashion has given us a simple mode of dressing the hair, which is well adapted to the average English head, and which is fully explained by the accompanying sketch. It may be taken as a safe rule, when the forehead is low and face small, that the hair may be drawn back with advantage, but a long face is generally improved by arranging the hair in soft curls on the forehead, and by waving it slightly at the sides, which adds to the apparent width of the countenance. But whatever style is in fashion, it is sure to have its admirers, for has not Pope left on record:

"Fair tresses man's imperial race ensnare, And beauty draws us by a single hair."

CHAPTER III.

GLOVES.

"Gloves as sweet as damask roses."--Shakespeare.

"See how she leans her cheek upon her hand. O, that I were a glove upon that hand, That I might touch that cheek."

--Romeo and Juliet.

The glove as an article of dress is of great antiquity, and among the fossils of the cave-dwellers of pre-historic times, which have been recently discovered in France, Belgium, and Switzerland, there is ample proof of its existence. Probably the first gloves were formed of skins, sewn with bone needles, and were long enough to reach above the elbow.

Xenophon, speaking of the Persians, gives as an instance of their effeminacy "that they not only covered their head and feet, but guarded their hands from cold by thick gloves." Homer, describing Lates at work in his garden, represents him with gloves on his hands to protect them from thorns. Pliny the younger, in speaking of his uncle's visit to Vesuvius, states that his secretary sat by ready to write down anything that was remarkable, and had gloves on his hands that the coldness of the weather need not impede his work. Varro, an ancient writer says:--"Olives gathered with the naked hand are preferable to those plucked in gloves;" and Atheneus speaks of a glutton who wore gloves at table so that he might handle the meat while hot and devour more than the others present.

That the Anglo-Saxons wore gloves we gather from their being mentioned in an old romance of the seventh century known as the "Poem of Beowulf," and according to the laws of Ethelred the Unready, five pairs of gloves formed part of the duty paid to that Prince by certain German merchants. In Planch?s "History of British Costume," an Anglo-Saxon lady appears to be wearing a glove with a separate division for the thumb but without fingers, and exactly resembling an infant's glove of the present day. In 1462 Edward IV. forbade the importation of foreign gloves to England, a law which remained in force till 1826.

In the early Christian Church gloves played an important part. In A.D. 790 Charlemagne granted an unlimited right of hunting to the Abbot and monks of Sithin, so that the skins of the deer they killed could be used in the manufacture of gloves, girdles, and covers of books. In some cases it was commanded that the clergy should wear gloves in administering the Sacrament, and a writer in the "Antiquary" states:--"It was always looked upon as decorous for the laity to take off their gloves in church where ecclesiastics alone might wear them. It was perhaps regarded as a proof of clean hands, for to this day persons sworn in our law courts are compelled to remove their gloves." In the ancient Consecration Service for the Bishops of the Church, a blessing was invoked on the gloves they wore. Those of William of Wykeham preserved at New College, Oxford, are adorned with the sacred monogram in red silk, and ecclesiastical gloves were often lavishly decorated with embroidery and jewels, and were bequeathed by will with other valuables.

Formerly judges were forbidden to wear gloves when engaged in their official duties, but are no longer bound by this restriction, and receive as a memorial of a maiden assize (that is, when there are no prisoners to be tried) a pair of white kid gloves from the sheriff, and during the time fairs were held their duration was marked by hanging a glove outside the town hall. As long as it remained there all persons in the place were exempt from arrest, but directly it was removed it was the signal for closing the fair, and the privilege was at an end.

Throwing down a glove was regarded as a challenge to combat, and this curious old custom is still retained in the English coronation ceremony. Kings were also invested with authority by the delivery of a glove. As un gage d'amour it has for centuries been esteemed, and in the days of chivalry it was usual for knights to wear their ladies' gloves in their helmets, as a talisman of success in arms. In old records we also meet with the term "glove money," a sum paid to servants with which they were to provide this portion of their livery, and till quite recently it was the custom to present those who attended weddings and funerals with gloves as a souvenir.

Shakespeare often mentions gloves, and some assert that he was the son of a glover. A pair which belonged to the dramatist is still preserved. They are of brown leather, ornamented with a stamped pattern, and are edged with gold fringe. They were presented by the actor Garrick to the Mayor and Corporation of Stratford-on-Avon at the Shakespearian commemoration in 1789.

Many royal gloves have found a place in private collections. Henry VI.'s glove has a gauntlet, is made of tanned leather, and is lined with deer-skin, and the hawking glove of Henry VIII. is another interesting relic of a bygone age. The King kept his hawks at Charing Cross, and in the inventories taken after this monarch's death we read of "three payre of hawkes' gloves, with two lined with velvet;" and again at Hampton Court there were "seven hawkes' gloves embroidered." The hawking glove, of which an illustration is given, may be seen in the Ashmolean Museum. It is of a simple character, evidently intended for use rather than ornament.

Gloves were not generally worn by women till after the Reformation; but during the sixteenth and seventeenth centuries their use gradually extended to the middle classes. Queen Elizabeth's glove may be seen at the Bodleian Library, Oxford, and is believed to have been worn at the visit of the Virgin Queen to the University in 1566. It is fringed with gold, and is nearly half a yard in length; it is made of white leather worked with gold thread, and the cuff is lined with drab silk. Mary Queen of Scots' glove in the Saffron Walden Museum is of light buff leather, wrought with silver wire and silk of different colours. It is lined with crimson satin, edged with gold lace enriched with sequins, and the opening is connected with bands of satin finished with lace insertion. This glove was presented on the morning of her execution to a member of the Dayrell family, who was in attendance at Fotheringay Castle. In happier days Queen Mary gave an exquisitely embroidered pair of gloves, with a design in which angels' heads and flowers appear--her own work--to her husband, Lord Darnley; and the gloves generally of the Tudor period were more ornate than those which adorn beauty's hands on the eve of the nineteenth century, and were, in most cases, wrought with the needle.

Though the history of gloves savours of romance, there is every reason to believe that they have sometimes been used with sinister motives, as a large trade was done at one time in poisoned gloves, delicately perfumed, to conceal their deadly purpose.

Some gloves which were the property of James I. are of brown leather lined with white, and the seams are sewn with silk and gold thread. The embroidery is in gold and silver thread on crimson satin, with a lining of red silk. They are finished with gold fringe, and have three loops at the side. A glove of chaste design, worn by Charles I. on the scaffold is made of cream-coloured kid, the gauntlet embroidered with silver and edged with silver fringe. Queen Anne, on the other hand, wore highly-decorated gloves of Suede kid, with raised silken flowers on the gauntlet, and three loops of rose-coloured ribbon, to allow them to be slipped over the hands. They are further enriched with gold lace and embroidery. A yellow Suede Court glove of George IV. gives the impression that the first gentleman of Europe had a fist of tremendous proportions. Her Majesty Queen Victoria generally wears black kid gloves, except for Court functions, when white glac?kid gloves are invariably used.

Her Royal Highness the Princess of Wales has a delicately-formed hand with tapering fingers, and her size is six and a-half. Her Royal Highness adapts her gloves to the occasion and toilette, and is always bien gant?

The first Napoleon gave an impetus to this branch of industry by insisting on gentlemen wearing gloves on State occasions and at festive gatherings, and the fashion spread through the countries of Europe with astonishing rapidity.

CHAPTER IV.

CURIOUS FOOT-GEAR.

"A tasteful slipper is my soul's delight."

--Milman's "Fazio."

A well-shaped foot has been considered from the earliest times one of Nature's kindest gifts, and sober history and fairy lore have combined to give us many interesting particulars respecting this portion of the human anatomy. The similarity of the foot-gear of both sexes makes it impossible to treat the matter separately, and as the subject is practically inexhaustible, I propose only to illustrate the most curious and notable examples.

One of the finest collection of shoes in the world is that at the Cluny Museum, Paris, formed by the eminent French engraver, the late Jules Jacquemart. This was enlarged by the purchase of the collection of Baron Schvitter. The Queen of Italy has also acquired a large number of historical boots and shoes; and to Mr. Joseph Box, another enthusiastic collector, I am indebted for some of the drawings used for illustrating this article.

A quaint story is told in a rare book, entitled "The Delightful, Princely, and Entertaining History of the Gentle Craft of Crispin, the Patron Saint of Shoe Makers, and his Brother Crispianus." According to this authority, they were the two sons of the King of Logia (Kent), and lived in the city of Durovenum, otherwise Canterbury, or the Court of the Kentish men. Having embraced

Christianity, during the Roman invasion, they were in considerable danger, and at their mother's instigation, to conceal their identity, adopted humble attire, and devoted themselves to the modest craft of shoemaking, under the auspices of a shoemaker at Faversham, to whom they bound themselves for seven years. This industrious citizen appears to have received the appointment of shoemaker to the Court of Maximinus, whose daughter Ursula fell in love with Crispin. After removing the usual obstacles (which, even in those remote times, seem to have obstructed the paths of those who had fallen under the sway of Cupid), this energetic lady engaged the services of a neighbouring friar, and cut the gordian knot by marrying her faithful adorer.

When primitive man first conceived the idea of producing some contrivance to defend himself from cold, sharp stones, or the heated sand of the desert, his first effort was to fasten to the bottom of his feet soles of bark, wood, or raw hide, which were followed, in due course, by more elaborately made sandals of tanned leather. These were fastened in various ways, but generally by two leathern straps, one round the instep, while the other passed between the first and second toes. Egyptian sandals were sometimes prolonged to a sharp point, and occasionally were made of papyrus, or some flexible material; but the commoner kinds were, as a rule, of wood or leather. Often they had painted upon them the effigy of the wearer's enemy, who was thus literally trodden underfoot. Owing to their proximity, the habits and customs of the Egyptians and Jews were in many respects similar. The same Hebrew word denotes both a sandal and a shoe; and it has been concluded that shoes were probably confined to the upper classes, while sandals were used by those compelled to work; and slaves went barefoot.

It will be seen from the sketches of Grecian and Roman shoes that they eventually became an elaborate article of dress, bound to the foot and leg with lacings, and ornamented in different ways. The senators had boots of black leather, with a crest of gold or silver on the top of the foot; and soldiers wore iron shoes, heavily spiked, in a similar manner to those now used for cricket, so as to give the wearers a better hold when scaling walls in the attack of fortified places. An iron boot was also used for torturing Christians. As an instance of the luxury so characteristic of the age, it is stated that Roman soldiers often had the spikes on their shoes made of gold. According to the testimony of Seneca, Julius Caesar wore shoes of the precious metal, a fashion emulated by Cardinal Wolsey many centuries after; and Severus was fond of covering his with jewels, to attract the attention of the people as he walked through the streets. The Emperor Aurelian forbade men to wear red, yellow, white, or green shoes, reserving these colours for women; and different shapes were prescribed by legal enactments to be worn for the easy distinguishment of various trades and professions. In the reign of Domitian, the stalls of shoemakers in the public streets were so numerous as to necessitate an edict for their removal.

Our own ancestors, the Anglo-Saxons, wore shoes of raw cow-hide, reaching to the ankles; and the hair turned outward. Those used by ecclesiastics were a kind of sandal fastened with bands of leather round the instep. The Norman half-boots had soles of wood, while the uppers were of a more pliable material. Those worn by the Crusaders were of chain, and later of plate armour. Very pointed toes were in fashion during the Middle Ages, and these were carried to such a ridiculous length that the dignitaries of the Church considered it necessary to preach against the practice. However, this did not result in its abolition, for we find the courtiers of the day improved upon the prevailing mode by stuffing their shoes, and twisting them into the shape of a ram's horn; the point of which was attached to the knee by a chain. The common people were permitted by law to wear "the pykes on their shoon" half-a-foot, rich citizens a foot, while nobles and princes had theirs two-and-a-half feet long.

During the Plantagenet period it was usual to wear two shoes of different colours, and they were often slashed on the upper surface, to show the bright hose beneath. These were superseded by a large, padded shoe, gored over the foot with coloured material, a fashion imported from Italy, and exaggerated as much as the pointed shoe had been. Buskins were high boots, made of splendid tissue, and worn by the nobility and gentry during the

Middle Ages, generally on occasions of State. They were also largely adopted by players of tragedy. They covered the knee, and were tied just below. The sock, or low shoe, on the other hand, was the emblem of comedy.

One of the greatest follies ever introduced was the chopine, a sort of stilt which increased the height of the wearer. These were first used in Persia, but appeared in Venice about the Sixteenth Century, and their use was encouraged by jealous husbands in the hope of keeping their wives at home. This desire, however, was not realised, as the ladies went out as usual, and required rather more support than hitherto. Chopines were very ornate, and the length determined the rank of the wearer, the noblest dames having them half-a-yard high. Shakespeare refers to them when he makes Hamlet say:--"Your ladyship is nearer heaven than when I saw you last by the altitude of a chopine." He also alludes to the general use of shoes for the left and right foot, when he speaks of a man:---

"Standing in slippers which his nimble haste Had falsely thrust upon contrary feet."

The exercise of the gentle craft of shoemaking was for a long time carried on in monastic institutions, and increased the revenues of the clergy. Richard, the first Abbot of St. Albans, objected to canons and priests of his era associating themselves with tanners and shoemakers, not one of whom, in his opinion, ought to be made a bishop or an abbot. It is said, however, that Pope John, elected in 1316, was the son of a shoemaker at Cahors; and in the description of Absalom, the Parish Clerk, Chaucer tells us, "the upper leathers of his shoes were carved to resemble the windows of St. Paul's Cathedral," which inclines one to believe in their priestly origin.

From various sources, we have descriptions of royal shoes. Richard C[oe]ur de Lion had his boots striped with gold; those of his brother John were spotted with gold in circles. Henry III. had his boots chequered with golden lines, and every square enriched with a lion. In the splendid Court of Edward III., the royal shoes were elaborately embroidered. The coronation shoes of

Richard III. were covered with crimson tissue cloth of gold. Henry VIII. is described as wearing square-toed shoes, which were slashed with coloured silk, and exposed a portion of the foot. Some worn by his daughter, Queen Elizabeth, of brocaded silk, are remarkably clumsy in appearance, and have lappets which fasten over the instep. They form a striking contrast to those used by the unfortunate Mary Queen of Scots (now in the possession of Sir James William Drummond), which are of kid, embroidered with coloured silks; the toes are somewhat squarer, but in other respects resemble those in fashion at the present day.

In speaking of curious foot-gear, the under covering of the leg and pedal extremities must be briefly referred to. Ancient works on costume frequently mention hose, socks, and stockings, which were made of woollen cloth, leather, or linen, and held in place by cross-bands of the material twisted to a little below the knee, either in close rolls, like the hay-bands of the modern ostler, or crossing each other sandal-wise, as they are now worn in some districts of Europe, particularly in Russia and Spain. Cloth stockings, embroidered with gold, are among the articles of dress ordered by Henry III. for his sister Isabel; and of a woman mentioned in the "Canterbury Tales," it is said: "Hire hosen weren of fine scarlet redde, ful streite yteyed (tied), and shoon full moist (supple) and newe."

In the reign of Henry VII. clocks on stockings are discernible; and the Poet Laureate of this king, describing the dress of the hostess of an inn, gives an indication of how boots were cleaned:

"She hobbles as she goes, With her blanket hose, Her shoone smeared with tallow."

It is supposed that hose or stockings of silk were unknown in this country before the middle of the 16th century. A pair of Spanish silk hose was presented by Sir Thomas Gresham to Edward VI., his father never having worn any but those made of cloth. In the reign of good Queen Bess, nether socks or stockings were of silk, jarnsey, worsted crewel, or the finest yarn, thread, or cloth, and were of all colours, "cunningly knit and curiously indented in every point, with querks, clocks, open seams, and everything else accordingly." Planch?states, in the third year of Elizabeth, Mistress Montague, the Queen's silk-woman, presented Her Majesty with a pair of black silk knit stockings, made in England; and from that time she wore no others, in the laudable desire to encourage their home manufacture by her own example. The Queen's patronage, and the invention, in 1599, of a weaving frame, by William Lee, Master of Arts, and Fellow of St. John's College, Cambridge, gave a great impetus tus to the stocking trade, which has been carried on with considerable success ever since, particularly in the Midland counties of England.

Spurs can be traced back to the Anglo-Saxon period, which is quite far enough for this purpose. They had no rowels, but were made with a simple point like a goad, and were fastened with leathers. Early in the 15th century spurs were screwed on to a steel shoe, instead of being fastened with straps. They were long in the neck, and the spikes of the rowels of formidable dimensions. From a sketch of a spur worn at the Battle of Naseby, in the reign of Charles I., it will be seen that, as progress was made in armour and military gear, considerable attention was paid to this portion of the soldier's outfit; indeed, it was more elaborate in design than is now considered necessary. From a very early period spurs have been used by both sexes.

A curious custom was in vogue at the beginning of the present century for ladies to make their own indoor shoes. This fashion was inaugurated by Queen Charlotte, who was particularly deft in handling a beautiful set of shoemaker's tools, mounted in silver, with ivory handles. Tradesmen bitterly complained that worktables in boudoirs were strewn with the implements of their craft; but, like many other feminine fads, it soon passed away. About this period clogs were also used. These were made of wood, and served as a protection to shoes out of doors. A similar contrivance, with the addition of an iron ring, leather strap and toe-cap, is still sometimes worn by farm servants, and is called a patten. Another form of clog, consisting of a laced leather boot with wooden sole, is extensively used by the working classes in the North of England, and the sabot, a wooden shoe, is the ordinary foot-gear of peasants on the Continent.

It is well known that Chinese women of high rank deform their feet by compressing them in such a manner that it is afterwards almost impossible to walk; and in Davis' interesting description of the Empire of China, he relates that whenever a judge of unusual integrity resigns his post, the people accompany him from his home to the gates of the city, where his boots are drawn off with great ceremony, and are afterwards preserved in the Hall of Justice.

In Japan a peculiar wooden sandal, having a separate compartment for the great toe, is in common use. Straw slippers are also worn, and a traveller starting on a journey will strap a supply on his back, so that he may have new shoes in case of need. They are lefts and rights, and only cost a halfpenny the pair. Here one never finds those deformities of the feet so common in China, and even in our own country. A graceful carriage depends so much upon the shoes worn. Heavy and stiff ones oblige the wearer to plant the foot solidly at every step. If the toes are very pointed it is at the sacrifice of elasticity, and if the heels are too high the muscles in the ball of the foot are little used.

Orientals indicate reverence by uncovering their feet, and do so on all occasions when Western nations would remove their hats. Their heads, being generally shaven, are always covered, and are surmounted by a head-dress which could not be replaced without considerable trouble; while for the feet they have loose slippers, with a single sole, made of coloured morocco or embroidered silk, which are easily thrown off. Few things inspire them with greater disgust than for anyone to enter their rooms with shoes on. They think such conduct an insult to themselves and a pollution to their apartment; and it is considered the height of irreverence to enter a church, mosque, or a temple without removing them. Even classical heathenism affords instances of this usage. The Roman women were obliged to go barefoot in the Temple of Vesta; the same rule existed in that of Diana, at Crete; and those who prayed in the Temple of Jupiter also followed this custom.

In the East, the public removal of the sandal or shoe, and the giving it to another, accompanied by certain words, signifies a transfer of authority or relinquishing possession. We are told in the case of Ruth and Boaz, when her kinsman gave up his right to marry her, in favour of her second husband, "he drew off his shoe." Among the Bedouins, when a man permits his cousin to marry another, or divorces his runaway spouse, he generally says, "She was my slipper; I have cast her off." Again, when shoes are left at the door of an apartment, they denote that the master or mistress is engaged, and even a husband does not venture into a wife's room while he sees the slippers on the threshold. The idea is not altogether unknown among ourselves, as it is expressed in the homely proverb, "to stand in another man's shoes;" or when we speak of coming into a future inheritance as stepping into a "dead man's shoe." Also in flinging the slipper after a departing bride, signifying that the father transfers his authority to the husband.

CHAPTER V.

BRIDAL COSTUME.

Certain curious customs have been associated with the Ordinance of Marriage from a very early period, and among others may be mentioned the union of near relations in barbaric or semi-barbaric tribes; the providing of husbands and wives for a family according to seniority (so that the younger members had to possess their souls in patience till the elder ones were disposed of); the paying of an equivalent for the bride's services to her father in money or kind; and festivities often lasting over several days to celebrate the nuptials. The Rabbins acquaint us with the fact that seven days' feasting was an indispensable obligation on all married men, and that the bride was not consigned to her husband until after the days of feasting had expired. They were generally spent in the house of the woman's father, after which she was conducted in great state to her husband's home. When the bride was a widow, the festivities only lasted for three days. Customs in the East are perpetuated from one generation to another, and we now find among the inhabitants of the Orient the same mode of life as was adopted by the patriarchs of old. The description of the wooing of Isaac and Rebekah, for example, so graphically told in Genesis, differs in few respects from that of a young couple of the same rank in the present day. Handsome presents, consisting of jewels, apparel, &c., are presented to the woman and her family, and form part of her dower in case of divorce. Rich shawls, fine dresses, personal ornaments, money, and a complete outfit of domestic utensils are always included in such a gift. Among some of the Arab tribes the dower received on such occasions, and called the "five articles," consists of a carpet, a silver nose ring, a silver neck chain, silver bracelets, and a camel bag. Matrimonial overtures are generally made by the parents of the contracting parties in Persia, but after all has been concluded, the bride-elect has nominally the power, though it is seldom exercised, of expressing her dissent before the connection receives its final sanction. Among many Bedouin tribes the woman is not suffered to know until the betrothing ceremonies announce it to her who is to be her husband, and then it is too late to negative the contract, but she is permitted to withdraw from her husband's tent the day after her marriage, and to return to her father; in which case she is formally divorced, and is henceforward regarded as a widow. On the value of her ornaments the Eastern bride bases her claim to consideration; and though the Arab, as a rule, cares little for his own dress, he decks his wife as richly as possible, that honour may be reflected upon himself and his circumstances. The leg ornaments and bracelets are often enormously thick, and have no fastenings, but open and compress by their own elasticity. It is not unusual to wear several on the same arm, reaching to the elbow. They form a woman's sole wealth, and are not treasured up for special occasions, as is usual among Western nations, but are used as part of of the daily costume. Various materials are employed in their manufacture; gold is necessarily rare, silver less so, while others are composed of amber, coral, mother-of-pearl, and beads.

We are told, when Rebekah approached her future home and saw a man walking in the distance, she evinced a curiosity, natural under the circumstances, and inquired about him; and on discovering that it was Isaac, "she took a veil and covered herself." It is still almost universal in the East for a woman, whose face is not concealed on other occasions, to envelop her head and body in an ample veil before she is conducted to her husband, and it is considered an indispensable part of the bridal costume. The details of the home coming are modified by the local usages and religions of the different countries. In Syria, Persia, and India, the bridegroom, in person, brings home the bride; in some other countries this duty devolves on a near relative, and he remains at home to receive the lady on her arrival. From various sources, but particularly from indications in Scripture, we may gather that the Jews employed either of these methods, according to circumstances. Again, in Egypt the bridegroom goes to the Mosque when his bride is expected, and returns home in procession after she has arrived. In Western Asia the procession usually walks, if the bride's future house is at no great distance in the same town. In such cases she is often partially covered by a canopy, and in Central and Eastern Asia it is the rule for her to be mounted on a mare, mule, ass, or camel, unless she is carried in a palanquin. Much, of course, depends on the social position of those married. Music attends such processions, and often dancing; the Jews certainly had the former, and some think the latter also, at least, in the time of our Saviour.

In Halhed's translation of the Gentoo Laws, and in Mr. Roberts's "Oriental Illustrations," reference is made to the custom of marrying the elder sister first, and the same usage is observed with regard to the brothers. When, in India, the elder daughter happens to be blind, deaf, dumb, or deformed, this formality is dispensed with; and there have been cases when a man, wishing to obtain a younger daughter, has used every means in his power to promote the settlement of his future sister-in-law, so as to forward his own nuptials. Fathers, too, will sometimes exert their powers to compass the marriage of the elder daughter, when a very advantageous offer is made for the younger one.

It is generally believed that Psalm xlv., commonly known as "The Song of Loves," was composed on the occasion of Solomon's marriage--probably to Pharaoh's daughter; and here we find the Egyptian bride's dress described as "all glorious within and wrought of gold, a raiment of needlework." Both expressions refer to the same dress, and imply that the garment was embroidered with figures worked with threads of gold. The Egyptians were famous for their embroideries, and some mummies have been found wrapped up in clothing curiously ornamented with gold lace. At the present day, both in Egypt and Western Asia, it is usual for ladies of the highest rank to employ much of their time in working with the needle linen and cotton tissues in gold and silver thread and silk of different colours.

The use of nuptial crowns is of great antiquity. Among the Greeks and Romans they wore chaplets of flowers and leaves, and the modern Greeks retain this custom, employing such chaplets, decorated with ribbons and lace. Modern Jews do not use crowns in their marriage ceremonies, and they inform us that they have been discontinued since the last siege of Jerusalem by the Romans. The information which Gemara gives on this subject is briefly that the crown of the bridegroom was of gold and silver, or else a chaplet of roses, myrtle, or olives, and that the bride's crown was of the precious metals. There is also some mention of a crown made of salt and sulphur, worn by the bridegroom, the salt transparent as crystal, the figures being represented thereon in sulphur. Crowns play an important part in the nuptial ceremonies of the Greek Church; they are also still used by Scandinavian brides.

The ring in former days did not occupy the prominent position it does now, but was given, with other presents, to mark the completion of the contract. Its form is a symbol of eternity, and signifies the intention of both parties to keep the solemn covenant of which it is a pledge, or, as the Saxons called it, a "wed," from which we derive the term wedding. The Jews have a law which proclaims that the nuptial ring shall be of certain value, and must not be obtained by credit or gift. Formerly they were of large size and elaborate workmanship, but now the ordinary plain gold hoop is used.

A wedding ring of the Shakespearian era has a portrait of Lucretia holding the dagger, the reverse side of the circle being formed by two clasped hands. This is a very common shape, and is shown in the illustration of the English wedding-ring E, dated 1706, where white enamel fingers support a rose diamond. The modern Italian peasant wedding-ring B is of gold in raised bosses, while C is of silver; F, bearing initials on vezet, is of bronze. A is a handsome Jewish wedding-ring, bearing the ark, and D also has a Hebrew inscription.

The gimmal betrothal ring was formerly a favourite pattern, and consisted of three circlets attached to a spring or pivot, and could be closed so as to appear like one solid ring. It was customary to break these asunder at the betrothal, the man and woman taking the upper and lower ones, and the witness the intermediate ring. When the marriage took place these were joined together and used at the ceremony. During the sixteenth and seventeenth centuries it was a common practice to engrave these emblems of affection with some appropriate motto. It was from Pagan Rome that European nations derive the wedding-ring, as they were used in their betrothals long before there is any trace of them elsewhere.

In describing the bridal costumes of different nations, it should be distinctly borne in mind that a large majority of the upper classes wear on such occasions the traditional white satin and orange blossoms with which we are all familiar. Many, however, prefer the picturesque national costume associated with the land of their birth, and it has been my principal object, in selecting the illustrations, to make them as typical as possible.

The Greek marriage service is full of symbol, and the sketch gives a good idea of the bridal costume. The bridesmaid is attired in a gold embroidered jacket, a skirt of brilliant colouring, and the crimson fez--the usual head-gear of a Greek maiden. She is depicted scattering corn, an ancient rite always performed at the conclusion of the ceremony. As she gracefully sways backwards and forwards, to the accompaniment of the jingling coins, which do double service as dowry and trimming, it is a pose and dress at once graceful and free. Formerly a wedding garment was often passed down from mother to daughter, and such an example is given in the soft yellow silk robe, lined with white and enriched with elaborate embroidery. Tiny stars in delicate shades of red, blue, and green, divided by black lines form the design and proclaim the industry and skill of the worker. These robes, however, have not been used in Greece since the beginning of the seventeenth century.

In Japan, the beautiful land of the lily and chrysanthemum, the bride usually takes little more to her husband's home than her trousseau, which is ample enough, as a rule, to satisfy even a woman's passion for dress. The nuptials take place in the evening, and the bride is garbed in virgin white robes, figured with a lozenge design. These garments are the gift of the bridegroom, and in them she passes from the home of her girlhood to that of her husband. The household gods of both families are assembled before an altar decked with flowers and covered with offerings. Near stands a large table, with a dwarf cedar; it also holds the Japanese Adam and Eve, and the mystic turtle and stork. The two special attendants of bride and bridegroom are called butterflies, and in their dress and colouring rival these beautiful insects, which in this country are the symbol of conjugal felicity. The most solemn part of the marriage ceremony is the scene of the two-mouthed vase. At a signal, one butterfly fills the vase, and the other offers it to the kneeling couple, the husband drinking first, and afterwards the wife. This draught signifies that henceforward they are to partake equally of the bitters and sweets of the coming years. Rice is thrown from either side, so as to mingle, and the wicks of two candles are placed together, to symbolize the joining of body and soul.

The marriage processions of other Oriental nations have already been referred to, and in India it is customary to perform the ceremony under a species of canopy richly ornamented and lighted by lamps. The bride wears, in addition to the native costume, a curious veil composed of strings of gold beads and tassels. In Hindu marriages the sacred fire or oman (which is constantly renewed by throwing upon it scented oils, sandalwood, incense, and other aromatic perfumes) is a prominent feature, and the union of a couple is consecrated by sprinkling a handful of saffron, mixed with rice flour, on their shoulders. Finally, the husband presents his wife with a little golden image called talee, a substitute for the wedding ring, and worn by Indian women as their symbol of matrimony.

A missionary thus describes a Buddhist marriage:--"The bride, loaded with jewellery, accompanied by women richly attired, entered the room, and sat down with the bridegroom on the floor. A number of candles were then lighted, and the company saluted and congratulated the happy couple, and expressed their kind wishes by blowing smoke towards them, while a band of string instruments discoursed sweet music. Two cushions were placed before the bridegroom, on which a sword was laid, and food was also near them. Next the hands of each were bound together, then the two to each other with silken threads. This act was performed by the nearest relative present, and completed the ceremony." Brief, indeed, are the forms of marriage indulged in by the people of Borneo. Each of the contracting parties chews a betel nut; an elderly woman mutters some sort of incantation, and brings the heads of bride and bridegroom in close contact, after which they are declared man and wife, and are no longer regarded as twain, but one flesh. The Cherokee form of marriage is perhaps the most simple. The two join hands over a running stream, emblematic of the wish that their future lives, hopes, and aspirations, should flow on in the same channel. A peculiar custom of the Lascars is the putting of a ring on the great toe when they marry. Mrs. Bishop, who has explored Tibet and studied the habits and customs of the people, informs us that polyandry is favoured by the women of that country. The heir of the land and eldest son appears to be the only member of the family who can contract a marriage in the legal sense as we understand it, but all his brothers are accepted by the wife as inferior or subordinate husbands. By this means they are kept well under the control of the superior husband, whom they regard as the "Big Father," and, as a matter of form, any children who may be born are accepted by him.

Thus the whole family are attached to the soil, and seem to work in concord, and the women have the satisfaction of knowing that in the average course of Nature they can never become widows, and that there will always be someone to work for them and their offspring. "It is the custom for the men and women of a village to assemble when a bride enters her home with her husbands, and for each of them to present her with three rupees. The Tibetan wife, far from spending these gifts on personal adornment, looks ahead, contemplating possible contingencies, and immediately hires a field, the produce of which is her own, and accumulates from year to year, so that she may not be portionless should she desire a divorce."

The African tribes, of course, differ materially in their marriage customs, but some form of exchange for the services of the woman are insisted on, and often take the shape of a present of cattle to the bride's father. On the West Coast, in the neighbourhood of Gaboon, where slavedom is recognised, there is an understanding that a wife may be purchased for a slave bundle, valued at about ? in English money, and there appears to be no sliding scale as to youth, beauty, form, or degree. A bundle contains specimens of every article sold by a general storekeeper. The most important features of a slave bundle are a Neptune, or brass pan used for making salt, which is a current article of commerce, and a piece of native cloth, manufactured by these people for dress purposes, from a species of palm which grows on the river banks in great luxuriance. Both sexes anoint themselves with palm oil and other greasy substances, and no greater compliment can be paid to an African belle than to say she looks "fat and shining."

Mr. Hutchinson, in his interesting work, "Ten Years in 苜 hiopia," gives a quaint and amusing account of the toilet of a Fernandian bridegroom: "Outside a small hut, belonging to the mother of the bride expectant, I soon discovered the happy bridegroom undergoing his toilet at the hands of his future wife's sister. A profusion of Tshibbu strings being fastened round his body, as well as his legs and arms, the anointing lady, having a short black pipe in her mouth, proceeded to rub him over with Tola pomade. He seemed not altogether joyous at the anticipation of his approaching happiness, but turned a sulky gaze now and then on a piece of yam which he held in his hand, and which had a parrot's red feather fixed on its convex side. This was called 'Ntshoba,' and is regarded as a protection against evil influences on the important day. The bride was borne down by the weight of rings and wreaths and girdles of Tshibbu. Tola pomatum gave her the appearance of an exhumed mummy, save her face, which was all white; not from excess of modesty, for the negro race are reported to blush blue, but from being smeared over with a white paste, the emblem of purity." What a hideous substitute for the classical wreath of orange blossoms, and what a contrast must be offered when the cosmetic peels off and displays the dusky skin upon which it is laid!

According to Russian law, no man can marry before he is eighteen years of age, or a woman before she is sixteen; nor after he is eighty, and she is sixty. Priests are permitted to marry once. Secret marriages without witnesses are regarded as invalid, and both bride and bridegroom must be baptized persons. If a Russian takes a foreigner for a wife, she must bind herself in writing to bring up any children she may have in the Greco-Russian faith. According to an ancient custom the bridegroom presents his bride with the costume and jewellery worn at the marriage. The dowry comes from her family, and consists of a complete wardrobe, silver, linen, and household furniture of all kinds. The hair of an unmarried woman of the peasant class in Russia is dressed in a single plait hanging loose upon the shoulders, and tied with ribbon. After marriage it is arranged in two braids coiled round the head, covered with a cap tied behind, or with a cotton or silk handkerchief and a little lappet of linen rests on the forehead, and is considered an inevitable symbol of marriage. Marriages are performed after banns, and much of the finery used by the lower classes is hired for the occasion; and the crowns used in the Russian ceremony are generally the property of the Church. Formerly they were worn for a week, but this practice has been discontinued.

There are three distinct periods in the life of a Norwegian woman, and each one has marked characteristics, particularly as regards dress. During girlhood, up to the time of confirmation, a solemn occasion for which there is much preparatory training, girls do not usually go from home to work, or earn their own living. Among the poorer classes this ceremony takes place when they are about fifteen. Their petticoats are short and their hair is arranged in two long plaits. After confirmation they are supposed to regard life from its more serious aspect, and to engage themselves with various duties, according to their station. The third stage, of course, is married life, and it should be stated that neither men nor women can enter upon the holy contract unless they can bring proof of their confirmation, and can show ample evidence of sufficient means to provide for a household. The marriage is preceded by a betrothal ceremony, when the young couple go to the church, accompanied by their friends, and exchange rings of plain gold and presents of jewellery and apparel, which must be worn on the wedding day. At her marriage the peasant bride wears the crown. It has a rim of brass to fit the head, and the upper portion is of silver and gold, sometimes embellished with precious stones. Such crowns are generally heirlooms, and it is not uncommon for all the brides of one family for centuries to wear the same adornment for the head. A very usual dress on such an occasion is a plain skirt of some woollen material, with a bodice and full sleeves of snowy linen, a corselet of red and green, ornamented with bands and buckles, and a white apron trimmed with embroidery. A silver-gilt breast ornament is worn by Swedish brides. The band is wrought with bosses, and depending from it are small beaten discs, and a medallion bearing the sacred initials I.H.S. The bridegroom's hat in the illustration was probably an heirloom too, from its shape and fashion. He wears a red waistcoat cut short and fastened with brass buttons, and a loose cloth coat ornamented with embroidered revers. The black small clothes show to advantage a well-shaped leg, and on the feet are low shoes. Usually the festivities in connection with a peasant wedding in Norway are kept up for three days, and during the time there is much feasting and merrymaking among the friends of bride and bridegroom.

Gipsies are, as a rule, married at a very early age. A girl is generally betrothed at fourteen, and becomes a wife two years later. The marriage ceremony is performed by a priest wearing a ram's horn as a sign of office, and, as becomes a nomadic race, the four elements--fire, air, earth, and water--take a prominent position. The horn is the symbol of authority, and is often made use of in Scripture. So much were rams' horns esteemed by the Israelites that their priests and Levites used them as trumpets in the taking of Jericho; and modern Jews when they confess their sins announce the ceremony by blowing a ram's horn. In ancient Egypt and other parts of Africa,

Jupiter Ammon was worshipped under the figure of a ram, and to this deity one of these animals was sacrificed annually. It seems to have been an emblem of power from the remotest ages. It would therefore appear that the practice of the gipsy priest wearing a ram's horn suspended from a string round his neck at a marriage is derived from the highest antiquity, and undoubtedly points to the Oriental origin of the gipsy race.

Various expedients have been resorted to by different rulers of sparsely populated kingdoms to encourage men to enter the married state. In ancient Rome the law forbade that a bachelor should inherit any legacy whatever, and in Sparta, under the rule of Lycurgus, they were not permitted to have a part in the government, nor might they occupy any civil or military post. They were excluded from participation in public festivals, except on certain fixed occasions, and then the women had the right to lead them to the altars, where they were beaten with rods to the sound of scornful songs. As late as the reign of William and Mary, widowers were taxed in England at the following rates:--Dukes, ?2 10s.; lower peers a smaller sum, and commoners one shilling each, if they elected to remain in a state of single blessedness. Widows also, especially those of high degree and fortune, were encouraged to dip again in the matrimonial lottery, and children were betrothed at a very tender age.

Bridesmaids in Anglo-Saxon times attended on the bride, and performed specified duties, particularly in the festivities which usually followed on such occasions. Even during the earlier portion of the present century it was a common custom for one to accompany the bridal couple on their honeymoon; and it was also her duty to prepare and present the "benediction posset," which is referred to by Herrick in "Hesperides:"--

"A short sweet prayer shall be said, And now the posset shall be made With cream of lilies not of kine And maiden blush for spiced wine."

The fashion of brides wearing spotless white is a comparatively modern one. From accounts of bridal gowns in bygone times, we find rich brocades, golden tissues, and coloured silks were employed for this purpose; and at the present day white is considered only appropriate to the virgin, and is absolutely dispensed with by those women who have been married before.

Of modern marriage customs in England there is no occasion to speak, for what woman is there among us who has not made an exhaustive and complete study of this vital matter? It may, however, comfort those who are beginning to wonder if marriage and giving in marriage is going out of fashion, to know that during the first quarter of 1894, 95,366 persons were joined together in the British Islands, an increase of 18 per cent. over the first three months of the previous year, 1893 and 9 per cent. over the mean rate for the same quarter for the preceding ten years. Figures are incontrovertible facts, so our ears need no longer be assailed by the bitter cry of

"DARKEST SPINSTERDOM."

CHAPTER VI.

MOURNING.

"The air is full of farewells to the dying And mourning for the dead."--Longfellow.

The signs of mourning in ancient times were by no means confined to the apparel. Fasting, laceration of the flesh, throwing dust on the head, and shaving the hair, were outward and visible signs of grief, accompanied by piercing cries of the most heartrending description. It was also customary to abstain from ornaments, to rend the clothing, and to put on filthy garments of sackcloth. This fabric was, and is still in the East, made of hair, which has an irritating effect upon the skin, and was for this purpose adopted as a penitential dress by the early Roman Church. The covering of the head was another manifestation of sorrow--a practice indicated by the hoods worn by female mourners, and the flowing hat-bands for men, so common at funerals a few years ago. In "A History of Mourning," by Richard Davey, from which many interesting facts on this subject may be gathered, we learn that the Egyptians, over three thousand years ago, selected yellow as the colour for mourning garments. The Greeks chose black as the most appropriate--a fashion followed by the Romans. The women of Rome had robes of black cloth, with veils of the same shade; but by a wise dispensation, young children were not compelled to adopt the symbols of woe. A year was the usual period for mourning a husband, wife, father, mother, sister, or brother; but relations who had been outlawed, imprisoned, or bankrupt, were not accorded this mark of respect. Numa published certain laws for the guidance of mourners, including one forbidding women to scratch their faces, or to make an exceptional display of grief at funerals. The Emperor Justinian (A.D. 537) also turned his attention to this subject, and regulated the expenses at funeral ceremonies, so as to secure those who remained from the double calamity of losing their friends and, at the same time, incurring heavy pecuniary liabilities on their account. Provision was made for burying each person free of cost, and for protecting the survivors from various extortions. Funds were appropriated for the purpose of interments, which were conducted by those appointed for the purpose. All persons were to be buried in the same manner; though those who desired to do so could, at their own cost, indulge in certain display, but this additional expense was limited. On state occasions, as, for example, on the death of an Emperor or a great defeat, the whole nation assumed the mourning garb. The defeat of Cann? the conspiracy of Catalina, and the death of Julius Caesar, were all considered of sufficient importance for the observance of this custom. Private mourning could be broken among the Romans by certain domestic events, as the birth of a son or daughter, the marriage of a child, or the return of a prisoner taken in war. Both sexes were expected to abstain from going to public ceremonies and places of amusement; and women were not allowed to marry till a year had elapsed from the husband's death, without the special permission of the Emperor. History, however, does not record that their lords and masters applied this rule to their own conduct.

The Greeks buried their dead before sunrise, so as to avoid ostentation. Mourning women took part in the procession, and accompanied the chief female mourner in her visits to the grave, on the seven days following interment. This custom, which was derived from the East, was a usual feature in Jewish, Roman, and Egyptian, as well as in Greek funerals.

The funeral feast was a common practice among the classical ancients, and was kept up to a comparatively recent period, in various European countries. The Cup of Consolation consisted of light refreshments prepared and sent in by the friends of mourners, who were not supposed to busy themselves with domestic affairs at such a time. The illustration gives a good idea of the mourning habit adopted by the immediate family of the deceased. Caves were used for the disposal of the dead, as well as elaborately constructed sepulchres, of which many remain to this day. Earth burial was in favour with some nations, but in time of war or pestilence cremation was resorted to. The practice of embalming we owe to the Egyptians, who carried it to a great state of perfection. One of the earliest embalmments on record is that of Joseph, whose body accompanied the Israelites on their journey through the Wilderness. He was placed in a coffin, a distinction in the East only accorded to those of the highest rank, the usual mode being to simply swathe the corpse closely in wrappers and bandages, thus retaining the shape of the human form. The Jews largely used spices and perfumes, which were employed both for anointing and for wrapping up the body--a very necessary precaution in hot climates. The Egyptians, on the death of a relative or sacred animal (the cat, for instance), attired themselves in yellow garments and shaved off their eyebrows. Their funeral processions were magnificent. When a king quitted this mortal sphere, the temples were closed for seventy-two days, and there were no sacrifices, solemnities, or feasts. Companies of two or three hundred men and women, in mean attire paraded the streets, singing plaintive songs and reciting the virtues of him they had lost. They ate no meat, or food dressed by fire, and omitted their customary baths and anointings. Every one mourned as for the death of a favourite child, and spent the day in lamentations. The Pyramids, those wonderful monuments to Egyptian monarchs, are memorials of the reverence and industry of the nation, whose high state of civilization is attested to by their works.

Burial clubs were common among the Anglo-Saxons, and heavy fines were inflicted on those who did not attend the funeral of a member. The corpse was placed on a bier, and on the body was laid the book of the Gospels, a code of belief and a cross as a symbol of hope. A silken or linen pall was used, according to the rank of the dead person. The clergy bore lighted tapers and chanted the psalter, the mass was performed, and a liberal offering made to the poor.

From a 9th century MS. in the National Library, Paris, is given a sketch which clearly defines the mourning habit of that period. The gown is evidently of black woollen cloth, trimmed with black and white fur; and a gauze veil of the same sombre tint envelops the head. From the same source a drawing of an Anglo-Saxon priest is given, on account of his wearing a black dalmatic, edged with fur, a vestment only adopted when a requiem mass was performed.

In the Middle Ages black was used for mourning as a rule, though purple and brown were occasionally substituted. Chaucer, in "The Knight's Tale," speaks of "clothes black all dropped with tears," and, again, of "widdowes habit of samite brown." In many cases, on the death of her husband, the wife retired for a year to a convent, when she assumed the nun's dress, of which the widow's weeds of the present day are a symbol. The mourning adopted by Katherine of Valois, wife of Henry V., the hero of Agincourt, who died at Vincennes in 1422, may be regarded as the typical widow's dress of that period. It consisted of a black brocade cote hardi, edged with white fur, and further embellished with black glass beads, which were also used for ornamenting the winged head dress. Her black woollen gown has a deep bordering of white fur. Some mourning habits of this period are represented in a splendid manuscript "Liber Regalis," still preserved in Westminster Abbey. They are composed of black fabrics in the prevailing fashion, and are furred with ermine. Froissart relates that the Earl of Foix, on hearing of the death of his son, Gaston, sent for his barber, and was close shaved, and clothed himself and his household in black. At the funeral of the Earl of Flanders, all the nobles and others present were attired in black gowns; and on the death of John, King of France, the King of Cyprus clothed himself in black mourning.

At the end of the fifteenth century, it was considered necessary in England to pass sumptuary mourning laws, owing to the extravagance of the nobility in the superfluous usage of cloth and other items at funerals. Habits and liveries were limited to certain quantities. Planch?tells us dukes and marquises were allowed sixteen yards for their gowns, sloppes (or mourning cassocks) and mantles; an earl, fourteen; a viscount, twelve; a baron, eight; a knight, six; and all inferior persons, two yards only; but an archbishop had the same privilege as a duke. Hoods were only permitted to those above the degree of esquire of the king's household.

Margaret, Countess of Richmond, the mother of King Henry VII., issued, in the eighth year of his reign, an ordinance for "the reformation of apparell for great estates of women in the tyme of mourninge." "They shall have their surcottes with a trayne before and another behynde, and their mantles with traynes. The queen is to wear a surcotte, with the traynes as aforesaid, and playne hoode, and a tippet at the hoode lying a good length upon the trayne of the mantell, being in breadth a nayle and an inche. After the first quarter of a year, the hood to be lined with black satin, or furred with ermine; and all ladies down to the degree of a baroness, are to wear similar mourninge, and to be barbed at the chin." The surcotte, with trayne, hood, barbe, and tippet, are visible in the sketch of a lady of the sixteenth century, taken from Pietro Vercellio's famous work on costume. The gentleman's mourning of black cloth and fur, is reproduced from a contemporary MS.

Among the obsolete funeral customs, may be mentioned the Death Crier, the lying-in-state of all classes, and the waxen effigies of those of royal rank. Before newspapers published obituary notices, it was customary for the Death Crier, armed with a bell and attired in a black livery, painted or embroidered with skulls and cross-bones, to announce to the townspeople, and inhabitants of surrounding villages, that another had gone over to the majority. This functionary was in the employ of the Corporation, or civil authorities, and on the death of a member of the Royal Family, he was usually accompanied by the Guild of Holy Souls, who walked in procession, bearing lighted tapers and other religious emblems. Lying-in-state usually lasted for three days, by which time the arrangements for a simple interment were completed, and the body was placed reverently in the ground. The obsequies of kings and queens, however, were carried over a protracted period, consequently a waxen figure was prepared, which was dressed in regal robes, and substituted for the body as soon as decomposition set in. This fashion was in vogue till the time of William and Mary, and in Westminster Abbey there is a collection of waxen effigies, which may be viewed by permission of the Dean. As likenesses they are interesting, and they are also useful as costume studies.

Of late years, in this country, mourning has been considerably modified, particularly for the male sex, who often content themselves with a black hat-band and another on the left sleeve of dark-coloured clothes. By Scotch law, whether a man dies solvent or insolvent, his widow may claim out of his estate, sufficient for mourning suitable to her rank, and the same privilege applies to each of her children, who are old enough to be present at their father's funeral. This right takes precedence over any debts the dead man may have contracted, and is a distinction not accorded to English, Welsh, or Irish widows.

In most European countries black is the accepted colour for mourning; though in different parts of the globe white, yellow, red, brown, and even blue garments are prescribed by custom as the emblem of death.

These shades have been selected for the following reasons:--Black is symbolical of the gloom which surrounds one when those who are nearest and dearest are taken. Black and white express sorrow mixed with hope, and white alone the light which follows the night of mourning. Blue, the tint of the heavens, to which it is hoped the spirit forms have taken flight. Yellow is typical of the dead autumn leaf, and brown the earth to which the body returns. Violet, a royal colour, is generally used for the mourning of kings and high dignitaries of the Church. Scarlet is also used for royal mourning occasionally.[A]

[Footnote A: For permission to reproduce some of the drawings from Davey's "History of Mourning," I am indebted to Messrs. Jay, Regent Street, London.]

CHAPTER VII.

ECCENTRICITIES OF MASCULINE COSTUME.

"The fashion wears out more apparel than the man."

--Much Ado about Nothing.

"Through tattered clothes small vices do appear, Robes and furred gowns hide all."--King Lear.

[Illustration: BRITON CLAD IN SKINS.]

[Illustration: BRITON AT THE TIME OF THE ROMAN INVASION.]

"Vanity, thy name is woman," "As vain as a woman," and similar epithets, are hurled at our defenceless heads by our teachers and masters; yet how few of them pause for a moment to consider whether they are altogether free from this human weakness or exempt from that love of dress which they so strongly condemn in others. It does not require a deep study of the history of costume to reveal some curious anomalies in this respect, and the sketches chosen for the purpose of illustrating this chapter will only give a faint idea of what has been considered appropriate and becoming to the manly form at different epochs. In Pelautier's "Histoire des Celtes," we learn that "the toilet of the ancient inhabitants of Britain, somewhat resembled that of the North American Indian of the present day, and consisted of a series of elaborate paintings over the whole surface of the body, which were no doubt originally intended to protect the skin, from the inclemencies of the weather, but were afterwards used as a mode of embellishment and a means of distinguishing the different classes, for it was reserved to freemen, and strictly forbidden to slaves. The lower classes confined themselves to small designs drawn at a considerable distance from each other; but the nobles had the privilege of ornamenting their persons with large figures, chiefly of animals, subsequently transferred to their shields, after they adopted a less scanty costume, and this may be looked upon as the origin of family arms." The Picts, who inhabited the north of Britain, were remarkable for their pictorial decorations, hence their name, derived from an ancient word, picti, which signifies painted. Our remote ancestors also added to their other charms (which were doubtless irresistible to the belles of that period), by deepening the tone of their naturally ruddy locks, by washing them in water boiled with lime. Their clothing was of skins of animals killed in the chase, and they were armed with implements of bone and flint. The Tyrian traders taught them how to construct various weapons of war from a composition of copper and tin, and their flat wicker shields were superseded by those of metal ornamented with concentric circles. After the Roman Conquest of Britain, the skin garments were laid aside for dyed tunics and close trousers. Over the tunic was worn a sagum, or short cloak, so named by the Romans from saic, a word of Celtic origin, which signified a skin or hide. When the head was covered it was with a cap, from the British cab, a hut, which, from its circular shape, it somewhat resembled, for the dwelling-places were composed of wattles firmly fixed in the ground and fastened together at the top. A curious remnant of this fashion is the horn-like cap of rushes still made by Welsh children. The hair was usually long and flowing. Men of rank shaved the chin and allowed the moustache to grow to an extraordinary length.

The Saxons and Danes are spoken of as wearers of "scarlet, purple, and fine linen," and the latter combed their hair once a day, bathed once a week, and frequently changed their clothing. By these means they found favour in the eyes of the women, and delighted the wives and daughters of the nobility. In a curious MS., written in the reign of King Canute, the monarch is represented in a tunic and mantle embellished with cords and tassels. The tops of his stockings are embroidered, but he wears simple leather shoes. A vestment presented by Canute to Croyland Abbey was of silk, embroidered with golden eagles, and the rich pall which he ordered to be laid over the tomb of Edmund Ironside, was "embroidered with the likeness of golden apples and ornamented with pearls." From this, we see that the needle played an important part in the ornamentation of clothing, and to it we also owe the splendid Bayeux tapestry, worked by Matilda, wife of William the Conqueror. This priceless curiosity is not only remarkable as a magnificent piece of workmanship, but affords a good idea of the dress of that period-- the 11th century. A tunic reaching to the ankle, leg bandages and shoes, a flowing mantle and flat cap, were the chief characteristics of the civil dress of this and succeeding reigns. The Normans, however, were clean-shaven.

During the Middle Ages extravagance prevailed in both male and female costume. Handsome furs were in great request, and several times sumptuary laws were passed. Men wore eight indispensable articles of dress, the shirt, breeches, stockings, shoes, coat, surcoat or cotehardie, mantle, and head dress. The coat or under-dress corresponded with the tunic of the ancients, and was entirely hidden, with the exception of the sleeves, by the surcoat. There were two kinds of mantles, one open in the front, the two sides connected by a strap resting on the chest, the other was open on the right side and had one end thrown over the left shoulder. Head coverings were of various descriptions; but many adopted hoods with long points, which were used to attach them to the belt when not in use. The assembling of Parliament in the reign of Richard II. gives the lay, spiritual, and legal peers in their usual costumes, and is reproduced from Planch?s "History of British Costume." The Bishops are in cowls near the throne, the judges in coifs and furred robes, the Earls of Westmorland and Northumberland stand in front. The Duke of Hereford, in high cap, is to the left of the throne, and Exeter, Salisbury, and other peers are seated opposite the judges. During the reign of Richard II., which lasted over twenty years (1377 to 1399), there were many curious fashions in masculine attire. The peaked shoes, chained to the knee, were not more ridiculous than the deep, wide sleeves commonly called pokeys, which were shaped like a bagpipe and were worn by all classes. Many writers refer to them as the devil's receptacles, as whatever could be stolen was hidden away in their folds. Some were wide and reached to the feet, others to the knee, and they were full of slits. Hose were often of different colours. Parti-coloured suits were also in favour, and these were frequently scalloped at the edges and embroidered with mottoes and other devices. Chaucer, who wrote the "Canterbury Tales" towards the end of Richard's reign, describes in the most graphic manner the apparel of his contemporaries. "The haberdasher, carpenter, weaver, dyer, and tapestry worker, all wealthy burghers of the City of London, were clothed in a livery, and the handles of their knives, pouches, and girdles were ornamented with silver. The clergy were not to be distinguished from the laity, and rode on horseback, glittering with gold, in gowns of scarlet and green, fine with cut work. Their mitres embellished with pearls like the head of a queen, and staffs of precious metals set with jewels." Even the parish clerk is said to be "spruce and foppish in his dress." The author of an anonymous work called the "Eulogium," of this date, says:--"The commoners were besotted in excess of apparel. Some in wide surcoats reaching to their loins, some in a garment reaching to their heels, closed before and sticking out at the sides, so that at the back they make men seem like women, and this they call by the ridiculous name gowne. Their hoods are little, and tied under the chins. Their lirri-pipes (tippets) pass round the neck, and hanging down before, reach to the heels."

Towards the end of the 14th century men began to wear short clothes made to fit the body so closely that it often required the assistance of two people to remove them, and it is from this period we can distinctly trace the difference between ancient and modern dress; in fact, our present fashions-- masculine and feminine--resemble to a certain extent those worn during medi鑒al times. Then, as now, men wore overcoats with tight sleeves, felt hats also with feathers, worn over a skull cap, and slung behind the back, and closely-fitting shoes and boots.

The Tudor monarchs paid considerable attention to the adornment of their persons, and were responsible for stringent legal enactments calculated to encourage home manufacturers. Felt hat-making--one of our oldest industries--was introduced into this country from Spain and Holland. A great impetus was given to this branch of trade by a law passed in 1571 which enjoined "every person above the age of seven years to wear on Sundays or holidays a cap of wool, knit made, thickened, and dressed in England by some of the trade of cappers, under the forfeiture of three farthings for every day's neglect." In 1603 the felt makers became a Corporation with grants and many privileges. Throughout the Middle Ages the upper classes frequently engaged in commerce. Bishops, abbots, and nobles personally superintended the disposal of the produce of their estates, and a considerable number of the younger sons of good families were the leading traders of the 15th and 16th centuries.

The "frocke" frequently mentioned, and of which the modern frock coat is the degenerate descendant, was a sort of jacket or jerkin made occasionally with skirts, a style associated especially, with Holbein's portraits of Henry VIII. and his contemporaries.

The uniform worn at the present day by the Yeomen of the Guard stationed at the Tower of London, gives us the military costume of the Tudor period. It is the oldest corps in her Majesty's service, and was instituted by Henry VII. as the bodyguard of the sovereign. In the dress of the Bluecoat Boys at Christ's Hospital we have that of the citizens of London during the reign of Edward VI. and Mary, when blue coats were habitually used by apprentices and serving men, yellow stockings also were in common use. The badges on the jackets of firemen and watermen date from this time; they were made of metal and placed on the sleeve, in the 16th century, instead of being embroidered on the back or breast of the garment as they had been previously. Retainers in the households of the wealthy, were provided with surcoats and mantles twice a year, of their patron's favourite colour, and this was called the livre, from a French word signifying to distribute. Trade guilds and members of the learned professions, also adopted a distinct style of costume. Lawyers, who were originally priests, of course wore the tonsure; but when the clergy ceased to interfere with secular affairs the lay lawyer continued this sign of office, and also wore a coif. Their gowns were capacious and lined with fur: and the Justices of the King's Bench were allowed liveries by the King, of cloth and silk. Budge, or lambskin, and miniver were provided for the trimming thereof, and the colour appears to have varied in different reigns, but for a long time green prevailed.

The courtiers of Elizabeth discarded the "frocke cote" for quilted and stuffed doublets and trunk hose, slashed and ornamented in the most quaint and extravagant manner. Below these were worn stockings embroidered with birds, beasts, and other devices, "sewed up close thereto as though they were all of one piece." Trunk hose were appropriately named, as they were often filled with wool, bran, and other materials. At last they became of such enormous size that it was necessary to construct swings in the Houses of Parliament in place of the ordinary fixed seats, for the accommodation of those wearing this singular article of attire. Enormous ruffs of muslin and lace encircled the necks of dandies of the Elizabethan era, and they appear to have had waists which would excite the envy of the belles of the latter part of the 19th century. In fact, the gallants of that day were even in advance of the fair sex, in their love of fantastic costume; and as Hollingshead, in The Chronicle, justly states in reference to the fashions of the period: "Nothing was more constant in England than inconstancy of attire."

A few years since, behind some ancient panelling at Haddon Hall, Derbyshire, was discovered a washing bill (with other things appertaining to the 16th and 17th centuries) which gives us a good idea of the various articles of dress then worn. Reference is made to the ruff, which is too well known to need description; to bandes made of linen and cambric, from which those now used by the clergy took their origin, and from which we derive the modern word bandbox. There were three kinds--some that stood upright, others were allowed to lie flat upon the shoulders, as shown in the drawings of Charles I. and II., and those which were embroidered and trimmed with lace. The shirt applied to the under-garment of both sexes, and the half-shirt referred to the stomacher over which the dress was laced. Boot hose were made of a variety of materials, and were occasionally called nether stocks; socks were sometimes put over them; and tops were of Holland linen or lace, and formed the lining of the full hanging boots of the Cavaliers.

During the Civil War the dress worn by the King's adherents, consisted of a doublet of silk or satin with loose sleeves, slashed up the front; the collar was generally of point lace, and a short cloak rested carelessly on one shoulder. The hat was a broad-brimmed beaver with a plume of feathers, and trunk hose gave way to breeches. The Roundheads or Republican Party went to the opposite extreme. They cut their hair close, avoided lace and jewels, had plain linen or cloth suits of a grey or brown tint, with a hat somewhat resembling the modern chimney pot.

* * * * *

About this period we also hear of the waistcoat, which was cut high at the neck, and was made with sleeves. Neckcloths and cravats of Brussels and Flanders lace were tied in a knot under the chin, and had square ends. Another peculiar feature of masculine costume towards the end of the 17th century consisted of petticoat breeches with drooping lace ruffles, such as adorn the nether limbs of Charles II. Patches and perukes were also adopted, and the former fashion, a revival of an old Roman custom, had political significance according to where they were placed on the face, and were bitterly ridiculed by numerous satirical writers. "I know many young gentlemen," says Middleton, in one of his plays, "who wear longer hair than their mistresses." The beard was worn in different ways, but the most usual shape was what Beaumont and Fletcher, in their "Queen of Corinth," call the T beard, consisting of a moustache and imperial:--

"His beard, Which now he put i' the form of a T, The Roman T; your T beard is the fashion, And two-fold doth express the enamoured courtier."

Shakespeare also tells us, it was often dyed different colours.

Everyone tried to rival his neighbour in the size of his peruke, till they became so preposterous that Charles II. showed his disfavour by writing a letter to the University of Cambridge forbidding the members to wear periwigs, smoke tobacco, or read their sermons. History does not relate what effect the King's censure had upon the head-gear of students attending the colleges, but it is absolutely proved that they paid no heed to his latter commands. It was the fashion for men to comb their perukes in public, and curiously-chased combs of bone and tortoise-shell, were carried in the pocket with the snuff-box, another indispensable appendage of a fine gentleman.

In the 18th century the broad hat brims were turned up at the sides, and, in the racy vernacular of the day, "each gallant cocked his hat according to his fancy." Shoe buckles became general in the reign of Queen Anne, and displaced the ribbon rosettes formerly worn. Planch?accurately describes the fashions of that day. "The square-cut coat was stiffened with wires and buckram, and the long-flapped waistcoat with pockets almost met the stockings. There were hanging cuffs with lace ruffles, square-toed shoes with red heels, and hats laced with gold or silver galloon."

At the beginning of the 19th century many important changes took place. Excepting for Court dress, cloth was substituted for velvet and other rich fabrics. The coat was open, displaying an elaborate shirt-front, stock and flowered waistcoat; and the skirt, though full, fell in natural folds. Trousers were very tight, and held in place by a strap beneath the foot, and hats displayed narrow curved brims.

We have only to cast our eyes down the vista of ages to find that British costume has been suited to the needs, habits, and customs of the people, and periods at which it was worn. Skins of animals were appropriate to the hardy cave dwellers who inhabited this country at an early period in the world's history. The simple dress of the Anglo-Saxons fulfilled the requirements of a primitive race; and the furs and rich fabrics brought home by the Crusaders were adapted to the higher state of civilization which prevailed in the Middle Ages. In the 16th century the Renaissance (of art and culture) was specially noted for richness of attire. During the 18th century a mixture of styles which had found favour with previous generations was the most marked feature in the costume of that period, and this equally applies to the two first decades of the present one. Masculine attire at the present day, though simple and practical, has few points of beauty to recommend it. Briefly, it resolves itself into a series of woollen cylinders which changeth not from generation to generation.

CHAPTER VIII.

A CHAT ABOUT CHILDREN AND THEIR CLOTHING.

"The childhood shows the man, As morning shows the day."--Milton.

Of children's dress in olden times we have singularly few details, and, as a rule, it may be concluded that their raiment was fashioned on similar lines to that worn by the men and women of the country in which they lived, and was more or less ornamented, according to their station in life.

One or two biblical references enlighten us as to Eastern customs. On the authority of St. Luke, our Saviour in infancy was wrapped in swaddling clothes. "Samuel," we are told, "being a child, was girded with a linen ephod," which appears to have been a close robe or vest reaching from the shoulders to the loins, and confined by a girdle. Considering the climate anand, to prevent prayer, Diabolous "lands up Mouthgate with dirt."2 Various efforts are made to send petitions, but the messengers make no impression, until, in the extremity of the soul's distress, two acceptable messengers are found, not dwelling in palaces, but in "a very mean cottage,"3 their names were "Desires Awake and Wet Eyes," illustrating the inspired words, "Thus saith the High and lofty One that inhabiteth eternity, whose name is holy: I dwell--with him--that is of a contrite and humble spirit" (Isa 57:15). By this we are taught the utter worthlessness of depending upon the prayers of saints on earth, or the glorified spirits of heaven. Our own prayers alone are availing. Our own "Desires-awake" and "Wet-eyes," our own aspirations after God, our own deep repentance and sense of utter helplessness drives us to the Saviour, through whom ALONE we can find access and adoption into the family of our Father who is in heaven.

The soul that communes with God attains an aptitude in prayer which no human learning can give; devotional expressions become familiar; the Spirit of adoption leads them with deep solemnity to approach the Infinite Eternal as a father. Private prayer is so essentially spiritual that it cannot be reduced to writing. "A man that truly prays one prayer, shall after that never be able to express with his mouth, or pen the unutterable desires, sense, affection, and longing that went to God in that prayer". Prayer leads to "pure religion and undefiled," "to visit the fatherless and widows in their affliction," and to preserve us "unspotted from the world" (James 1:27). Blessed indeed are those who enjoy an abiding sense of the Divine presence; the Christian's divine life may be measured by his being able to "pray without ceasing," to "seek God's face continually." Men ought "always to pray," and to "continue in prayer." This does not consist in perpetually repeating any form of prayer, but in that devotional frame of mind which enables the soul to say, "For me to live is Christ." When David was compassed about with the sorrows of hell, he at once ejaculates, "O Lord, I beseech thee deliver my soul." When the disciples were in danger they did not recite the Lord's Prayer, or any other form, but at once cried, "Lord, save us, we perish." Bunyan, speaking of private prayer, keenly inquires, will God not hear thee "except thou comest before him with some eloquent oration?" "It is not, as many take it to be, even a few babbling, prating, complimentary expressions, but a sensible feeling in the heart." Sincerity and a dependence upon the mediatorial office of Christ is all that God requires. "The Lord is nigh unto all them that call upon him--IN TRUTH" (Psa 145:18). In all that related to the individual approach of the spirit to its heavenly Father, our pious author offended not; but having enjoyed communion with God, he was, as all Christians are, desirous of communion with the saints on earth, and in choosing the forms of public worship, he gave great offence to many by rejecting the Book of Common Prayer.

To compel or to bribe persons to attend religious services is unjustifiable, and naturally produces hypocrisy and persecution. So it was with the decree of King Darius, (Dan 6); and so it has ever been with any royal or parliamentary interference with Christian liberty. "Who art thou that judgest another man's servant? to his own master he standeth or falleth" (Rom 14:4). "EVERY ONE of us shall give account of himself to God" (Rom 14:12). All the solemnities of the day of judgment point not merely to the right, but to the necessity of private decision on all questions of faith, worship, and conduct, guided solely by the volume of inspiration. Mansoul, in its regenerate state, is the temple which the Creator has chosen for his worship; and it is infinitely more glorious than earthly edifices, which crumble into dust, while God's temples will be ever glorious as eternity rolls on.

Bunyan, to the sixteenth year of his age, had, when he attended public worship, listened to the Book of Common Prayer. At that time an Act of Parliament prohibited its use under severe and unjust penalties, and ordered the services to be conducted by the rules of a directory. In this an outline is given of public thanksgivings, confessions, and petitions; but no form of prayer. In the preface the Puritans record their opinion, that the Liturgy of the Church of England, notwithstanding all the pains and religious intentions of its compilers, hath proved an offence; unprofitable ceremonies hath occasioned much mischief; its estimation hath been raised by prelates, as if there were no other way of worship; making it an idol to the ignorant and superstitious, a matter of endless strife, and of increasing an idle ministry. Bunyan had weighed these observations, and recollected his former ignorance and superstition, when he counted all things holy connected with the outward forms, and did "very devoutly say and sing as others did."4 But when he arose from the long and dread conflict with sin, and entered upon his Christian life, he decidedly preferred emancipation from forms of prayer, and treated them with great severity. He considered that the most essential qualification for the Christian ministry is the gift of prayer. Upon this subject learned and pious men have differed; but the opinions of one so eminently pious, and so well-taught in the Scriptures, are worthy of our careful investigation. Great allowances must be made for all that appears harsh in language, because urbanity was not the fashion of that day in religious controversy. He had been most cruelly imprisoned, with threats of transportation, and even an ignominious death, for refusing conformity to the Book of Common Prayer. Being conscientiously and prayerfully decided in his judgment, he set all these threats at defiance, and boldly, at the risk of his life, published this treatise, while yet a prisoner in Bedford jail; and it is a clear, concise, and scriptural discourse, setting forth his views upon this most important subject.

Any preconceived form would have fettered Bunyan's free spirit; he was a giant in prayer, and commanded the deepest reverence while leading the public devotions of the largest congregations. The great question as to public prayer is whether the minister should, relying upon Divine assistance, offer up prayer to God in the Saviour's name, immediately conceived under a sense of His presence; or whether it is better, as it is certainly easier, to read a form of prayer, from time to time, skillfully arranged, and with every regard to beauty of language? Which of these modes is most in accordance with the directions of the Sacred Scriptures, and most likely to be attended with spiritual benefit to the assembled church? Surely this inquiry does not involve the charge of schism or heresy upon either party. "Let every man be fully persuaded in his own mind." Nor should such differences lead us to despise each other. Let our first inquiry be, whether the Saviour intended a fixed form of prayer? And if so, did he give His church any other than that most beautiful and comprehensive form called the Lord's Prayer? And did he license any one, and if so, who, to alter, add to, or diminish from it? On the other hand, should we conclude that "We know not what we should pray for as we ought, only as the Spirit helpeth our infirmities," then must we rely, as Bunyan did, upon the promised aid of that gracious Spirit. Blessed, indeed, are those whose intercourse with heaven sheds an influence on their whole conduct, gives them abundance of well-arranged words in praying with their families and with the sick or dejected, and--whose lives prove that they have been with Jesus, and are taught by him, or who, in Scripture language, "pray with the spirit and with the understanding also."

GEO. OFFOR.

ON PRAYING IN THE SPIRIT.

"I WILL PRAY WITH THE SPIRIT, AND I WILL PRAY WITH THE UNDERSTANDING ALSO"--(I Cor 14:15).

PRAYER is an ORDINANCE of God, and that to be used both in public and private; yea, such an ordinance as brings those that have the spirit of supplication into great familiarity with God; and is also so prevalent in action, that it getteth of God, both for the person that prayeth, and for them that are prayed for, great things.5 It is the opener of the heart of God, and a means by which the soul, though empty, is filled. By prayer the Christian can open his heart to God, as to a friend, and obtain fresh testimony of God's friendship to him. I might spend many words in distinguishing between public and private prayer; as also between that in the heart, and that with the vocal voice. Something also might be spoken to distinguish between the gifts and graces of prayer; but eschewing this method, my business shall be at this time only to show you the very heart of prayer, without which, all your lifting up, both of hands, and eyes, and voices, will be to no purpose at all. "I will pray with the Spirit."

The method that I shall go on in at this time shall be, FIRST. To show you what true prayer is. SECOND. To show you what it is to pray with the Spirit. THIRD. What it is to pray with the Spirit and understanding also. And so, FOURTHLY. To make some short use and application of what shall be spoken.

WHAT PRAYER IS.

FIRST, What [true] prayer is. Prayer is a sincere, sensible, affectionate pouring out of the heart or soul to God, through Christ, in the strength and assistance of the Holy Spirit, for such things as God hath promised, or according to the Word, for the good of the church, with submission, in faith, to the will of God.

In this description are these seven things. First, It is a sincere; Second, A sensible; Third, An affectionate, pouring out of the soul to God, through Christ; Fourth, By the strength or assistance of the Spirit; Fifth, For such things as God hath promised, or, according to his word; Sixth, For the good of the church; Seventh, With submission in faith to the will of God.

First. For the first of these, it is a SINCERE pouring out of the soul to God. Sincerity is such a grace as runs through all the graces of God in us, and through all the actings of a Christian, and hath the sway in them too, or else their actings are not any thing regarded of God, and so of and in prayer, of which particularly David speaks, when he mentions prayer. "I cried unto him," the Lord "with my mouth, and he was extolled with my tongue. If I regard iniquity in my heart, the Lord will not hear" my prayer (Psa 66:17,18). Part of the exercise of prayer is sincerity, without which God looks not upon it as prayer in a good sense (Psa 16:1-4). Then "ye shall seek me and find me, when ye shall search for me with all your heart" (Jer 29:12-13). The want of this made the Lord reject their prayers in Hosea 7:14, where he saith, "They have not cried unto me with their heart," that is, in sincerity, "when they howled upon their beds." But for a pretence, for a show in hypocrisy, to be seen of men, and applauded for the same, they prayed. Sincerity was that which Christ commended in Nathaniel, when he was under the fig tree. "Behold, an Israelite indeed, in whom is no guile." Probably this good man was pouring out of his soul to God in prayer under the fig tree, and that in a sincere and unfeigned spirit before the Lord. The prayer that hath this in it as one of the principal ingredients, is the prayer that God looks at. Thus, "The prayer of the upright is his delight" (Prov 15:8).

And why must sincerity be one of the essentials of prayer which is accepted of God, but because sincerity carries the soul in all simplicity to open its heart to God, and to tell him the case plainly, without equivocation; to condemn itself plainly, without dissembling; to cry to God heartily, without complimenting. "I have surely heard Ephraim bemoaning himself thus; Thou has chastised me, and I was chastised, as a bullock unaccustomed to the yoke" (Jer 31:18). Sincerity is the same in a corner alone, as it is before the face of the world. It knows not how to wear two vizards, one for an appearance before men, and another for a short snatch in a corner; but it must have God, and be with him in the duty of prayer. It is not lip-labour that it doth regard, for it is the heart that God looks at, and that which sincerity looks at, and that which prayer comes from, if it be that prayer which is accompanied with sincerity.

Second. It is a sincere and SENSIBLE pouring out of the heart or soul. It is not, as many take it to be, even a few babbling, prating, complimentary expressions, but a sensible feeling there is in the heart. Prayer hath in it a sensibleness of diverse things; sometimes sense of sin, sometimes of mercy received, sometimes of the readiness of God to give mercy, &c.

1. A sense of the want of mercy, by reason of the danger of sin. The soul, I say, feels, and from feeling sighs, groans, and breaks at the heart. For right prayer bubbleth out of the heart when it is overpressed with grief and bitterness, as blood is forced out of the flesh by reason of some heavy burden that lieth upon it (I Sam 1:10; Psa 69:3). David roars, cries, weeps, faints at heart, fails at the eyes, loseth his moisture, &c., (Psa 38:8-10). Hezekiah mourns like a dove (Isa 38:14). Ephraim bemoans himself (Jer 31:18). Peter weeps bitterly (Matt 26:75). Christ hath strong cryings and tears (Heb 5:7). And all this from a sense of the justice of God, the guilt of sin, the pains of hell and destruction. "The sorrows of death compassed me, and the pains of hell gat hold upon me: I found trouble and sorrow." Then cried I unto the Lord (Psa 116:3,4). And in another place, "My sore ran in the night" (Psa 77:2). Again, "I am bowed down greatly; I go mourning all the day long" (Psa 38:6). In all these instances, and in hundreds more that might be named, you may see that prayer carrieth in it a sensible feeling disposition, and that first from a sense of sin.

2. Sometimes there is a sweet sense of mercy received; encouraging, comforting, strengthening, enlivening, enlightening mercy, &c. Thus David pours out his soul, to bless, and praise, and admire the great God for his loving-kindness to such poor vile wretches. "Bless the Lord, O my soul; and all that is within me bless his holy name. Bless the Lord, O my soul, and forget not all his benefits.6 Who forgiveth all thine iniquities, who healeth all thy diseases; who redeemeth thy life from destruction; who crowneth thee with

loving-kindness and tender mercies; who satisfieth thy mouth with good things, so that thy youth is renewed like the eagle's" (Psa 103:1-5). And thus is the prayer of saints sometimes turned into praise and thanksgiving, and yet are prayers still. This is a mystery; God's people pray with their praises, as it is written, "Be careful for nothing, but in every thing by prayer, and supplication, with thanksgiving, let your request be made known unto God" (Phil 4:6). A sensible thanksgiving, for mercies received, is a mighty prayer in the sight of God; it prevails with him unspeakably.

3. In prayer there is sometimes in the soul a sense of mercy to be received. This again sets the soul all on a flame. "Thou, O lord of hosts," saith David, "hast revealed to thy servant, saying I will build thee an house; therefore hath thy servant found in his heart to pray--unto thee" (II Sam 7:27). This provoked Jacob, David, Daniel, with others--even a sense of mercies to be received-- which caused them, not by fits and starts, nor yet in a foolish frothy way, to babble over a few words written in a paper; but mightily, fervently, and continually, to groan out their conditions before the Lord, as being sensible, sensible, I say, of their wants, their misery, and the willingness of God to show mercy (Gen 32:10,11; Dan 9:3,4).

A good sense of sin, and the wrath of God, with some encouragement from God to come unto him, is a better Common-prayer-book than that which is taken out of the Papistical mass-book,7 being the scraps and fragments of the devices of some popes, some friars, and I wot not what.

Third. Prayer is a sincere, sensible, and an AFFECTIONATE pouring out of the soul to God. O! the heat, strength, life, vigour, and affection, that is in right prayer! "As the hart panteth after the water-brooks, so panteth my soul after thee, O God" (Psa 42:1). "I have longed after thy precepts" (Psa 119:40). "I have longed for thy salvation" (ver 174). "My soul longeth, yea, even fainteth, for the courts of the Lord; my heart and my flesh crieth out for the living God" (Psa 84:2). "My soul breaketh for the longing that it hath unto thy judgments at all times" (Psa 119:20). Mark ye here, "My soul longeth," it longeth, it longeth, &c. O what affection is here discovered in prayer! The like you have in Daniel. "O Lord, hear; O Lord, forgive; O Lord, hearken and do; defer not, for thine own sake, O my God" (Dan 9:19). Every syllable carrieth a mighty vehemency in it. This is called the fervent, or the working prayer, by James. And so again, "And being in an agony, he prayed more earnestly" (Luke 22:44). Or had his affections more and more drawn out after God for his helping hand. O! How wide are the most of men with their prayers from this prayer, that is, PRAYER in God's account! Alas! The greatest part of men make no conscience at all of the duty; and as for them that do, it is to be feared that many of them are very great strangers to a sincere, sensible, and affectionate pouring out their hearts or souls to God; but even content themselves with a little lip-labour and bodily exercise, mumbling over a few imaginary prayers. When the affections are indeed engaged in prayer, then, then the whole man is engaged, and that in such sort, that the soul will spend itself to nothing, as it were, rather than it will go without that good desired, even communion and solace with Christ. And hence it is that the saints have spent their strengths, and lost their lives, rather than go without the blessing (Psa 69:3; 38:9,10; Gen 32:24,26).

All this is too, too evident by the ignorance, profaneness, and spirit of envy, that reign in the hearts of those men that are so hot for the forms, and not the power of praying. Scarce one of forty among them know what it is to be born again, to have communion with the Father through the Son; to feel the power of grace sanctifying their hearts: but for all their prayers, they still live cursed, drunken, whorish, and abominable lives, full of malice, envy, deceit, persecuting of the dear children of God. O what a dreadful after-clap is coming upon them! which all their hypocritical assembling themselves together, with all their prayers, shall never be able to help them against, or shelter them from.

Again, It is a pouring out of the heart or soul. There is in prayer an unbosoming of a man's self, an opening of the heart to God, an affectionate pouring out of the soul in requests, sighs, and groans. "All my desire is before thee," saith David, "and my groaning is not hid from thee" (Psa 38:9). And again, "My soul thirsteth for God, for the living God. When shall I come and appear before God? When I remember these things, I pour out my soul in me" (Psa 42:2,4). Mark, "I pour out my soul." It is an expression signifying, that in prayer there goeth the very life and whole strength to God. As in another place, "Trust in him at all times; ye people,--pour out your heart before him" (Psa 62:8). This is the prayer to which the promise is made, for the delivering of a poor creature out of captivity and thralldom. "If from thence thou shalt seek the Lord thy God, thou shalt find him, if thou seek him with all thy heart and with all thy soul" (Deut 4:29).

Again, It is a pouring out of the heart or soul TO GOD. This showeth also the excellency of the spirit of prayer. It is the great God to which it retires. "When shall I come and appear before God?" And it argueth, that the soul that thus prayeth indeed, sees an emptiness in all things under heaven; that in God alone there is rest and satisfaction for the soul. "Now she that is a widow indeed, and desolate, trusteth in God" (I Tim 5:5). So saith David, "In thee, O Lord, do I put my trust; let me never be put to confusion. Deliver me in thy righteousness, and cause me to escape; incline thine ear to me, and save me. Be thou my strong habitation, whereunto I may continually resort:--for thou art my rock and my fortress; deliver me, O my God,--out of the hand of the unrighteous and cruel man. For thou art my hope, O Lord God, thou art my trust from my youth" (Psa 71:1-5). Many in a wording way speak of God; but right prayer makes God his hope, stay, and all. Right prayer sees nothing substantial, and worth the looking after, but God. And that, as I said before, it doth in a sincere, sensible, and affectionate way.

Again, It is a sincere, sensible, affectionate pouring out of the heart or soul to God, THROUGH CHRIST. This through Christ must needs be added, or else it is to be questioned, whether it be prayer, though in appearance it be never so eminent or eloquent.

Christ is the way through whom the soul hath admittance to God, and without whom it is impossible that so much as one desire should come into the ears of the Lord of Sabaoth (John 14:6). "If ye shall ask anything in my name"; "whatsoever ye shall ask the Father in my name, I will do it" (John

14:13,14). This was Daniel's way in praying for the people of God; he did it in the name of Christ. "Now therefore, O our God, hear the prayer of thy servant, and his supplications, and cause thy face to shine upon thy sanctuary that is desolate, for the Lord's sake" (Dan 9:17). And so David, "For thy name's sake," that is, for thy Christ's sake, "pardon mine iniquity, for it is great" (Psa 25:11). But now, it is not every one that maketh mention of Christ's name in prayer, that doth indeed, and in truth, effectually pray to God in the name of Christ, or through him. This coming to God through Christ is the hardest part that is found in prayer. A man may more easily be sensible of his works, ay, and sincerely too desire mercy, and yet not be able to come to God by Christ. That man that comes to God by Christ, he must first have the knowledge of him; "for he that cometh to God, must believe that he is" (Heb 11:6). And so he that comes to God through Christ, must be enabled to know Christ. Lord, saith Moses, "show me now thy way, that I may know thee" (Exo 33:13).

This Christ, none but the Father can reveal (Matt 11:27). And to come through Christ, is for the soul to be enabled of God to shroud itself under the shadow of the Lord Jesus, as a man shroudeth himself under a thing for safeguard (Matt 16:16).8 Hence it is that David so often terms Christ his shield, buckler, tower, fortress, rock of defence, &c., (Psa 18:2; 27:1; 28:1). Not only because by him he overcame his enemies, but because through him he found favour with God the Father. And so he saith to Abraham, "Fear not, I am thy shield," &c., (Gen 15:1). The man then that comes to God through Christ, must have faith, by which he puts on Christ, and in him appears before God. Now he that hath faith is born of God, born again, and so becomes one of the sons of God; by virtue of which he is joined to Christ, and made a member of him (John 3:5,7; 1:12). And therefore, secondly he, as a member of Christ, comes to God; I say, as a member of him, so that God looks on that man as a part of Christ, part of his body, flesh, and bones, united to him by election, conversion, illumination, the Spirit being conveyed into the heart of that poor man by God (Eph 5:30). So that now he comes to God in Christ's merits, in his blood, righteousness, victory, intercession, and so stands before him, being "accepted in his Beloved" (Eph 1:6). And because this poor creature is thus a member of the Lord Jesus, and under this consideration hath admittance to come to God; therefore, by virtue of this union also, is the Holy Spirit conveyed into him, whereby he is able to pour out himself, to wit, his soul, before God, with his audience. And this leads me to the next, or fourth particular.

Fourth. Prayer is a sincere, sensible, affectionate, pouring out of the heart or soul to God through Christ, by the strength or ASSISTANCE OF THE SPIRIT. For these things do so depend one upon another, that it is impossible that it should be prayer, without there be a joint concurrence of them; for though it be never so famous, yet without these things, it is only such prayer as is rejected of God. For without a sincere, sensible, affectionate pouring out of the heart to God, it is but lip-labour; and if it be not through Christ, it falleth far short of ever sounding well in the ears of God. So also, if it be not in the strength and assistance of the Spirit, it is but like the sons of Aaron, offering with strange fire (Lev 10:1,2). But I shall speak more to this under the second head; and therefore in the meantime, that which is not petitioned through the teaching and assistance of the Spirit, it is not possible that it should be "according to the will of God" (Rom 8:26,27).

Fifth. Prayer is a sincere, sensible, affectionate pouring out of the heart, or soul, to God, through Christ, in the strength and assistance of the Spirit, FOR SUCH THINGS AS GOD HATH PROMISED, &c., (Matt 6:6-8). Prayer it is, when it is within the compass of God's Word; and it is blasphemy, or at best vain babbling, when the petition is beside the book. David therefore still in his prayer kept his eye on the Word of God. "My soul," saith he, "cleaveth to the dust; quicken me according to thy word." And again, "My soul melteth for heaviness, strengthen thou me according unto thy word" (Psa 119:25-28; see also 41, 42, 58, 65, 74, 81, 82, 107, 147, 154, 169, 170). And, "remember thy word unto thy servant, upon which thou hast caused me to hope" (ver 49). And indeed the Holy Ghost doth not immediately quicken and stir up the heart of the Christian without, but by, with, and through the Word, by bringing that to the heart, and by opening of that, whereby the man is provoked to go to the Lord, and to tell him how it is with him, and also to argue, and supplicate, according to the Word; thus it was with Daniel, that mighty prophet of the Lord. He understanding by books that the captivity of the children of Israel was hard at an end; then, according unto that word, he maketh his prayer to God. "I Daniel," saith he, "understood by books," viz., the writings of Jeremiah, "the number of the years whereof the word of the Lord came to Jeremiah,--that he would accomplish seventy years in the desolations of Jerusalem. And I set my face to the Lord God, to seek by prayer and supplications, with fasting, and sackcloth, and ashes" (Dan 9:2,3). So that I say, as the Spirit is the helper and the governor of the soul, when it prayeth according to the will of God; so it guideth by and according to, the Word of God and his promise. Hence it is that our Lord Jesus Christ himself did make a stop, although his life lay at stake for it. I could now pray to my Father, and he should give me more than twelve legions of angels; but how then must the scripture be fulfilled that thus it must be? (Matt 26:53,54). As who should say, Were there but a word for it in the scripture, I should soon be out of the hands of mine enemies, I should be helped by angels; but the scripture will not warrant this kind of praying, for that saith otherwise. It is a praying then according to the Word and promise. The Spirit by the Word must direct, as well in the manner, as in the matter of prayer. "I will pray with the Spirit, and I will pray with the understanding also" (I Cor 14:15). But there is no understanding without the Word. For if they reject the word of the Lord, "what wisdom is in them?" (Jer 8:9).

Sixth. FOR THE GOOD OF THE CHURCH. This clause reacheth in whatsoever tendeth either to the honour of God, Christ's advancement, or his people's benefit. For God, and Christ, and his people are so linked together that if the good of the one be prayed for, to wit, the church, the glory of God, and advancement of Christ, must needs be included. For as Christ is in the Father, so the saints are in Christ; and he that toucheth the saints, toucheth the apple of God's eye; and therefore pray for the peace of Jerusalem, and you pray for all that is required of you. For Jerusalem will never be in perfect peace until she be in heaven; and there is nothing that Christ doth more desire than to have her there. That also is the place that God through Christ hath given to her. He then that prayeth for the peace and good of Zion, or the church, doth ask that in prayer which Christ hath purchased with his blood; and also that which the Father hath given to him as the price thereof. Now he that prayeth for this, must pray for abundance of grace for the church, for help against all its temptations; that God would let nothing be too hard for it; and that all things might work together for its good, that God would keep them blameless and harmless, the sons of God, to his glory, in the midst of a crooked and perverse nation. And this is the substance of Christ's own prayer in John 17. And all Paul's prayers did run that way, as one of his prayers doth eminently show. "And this I pray, that your love may abound yet more and more in knowledge, and in all judgment; that ye may approve things that are excellent; that ye may be sincere, and without offence, till the day of Christ. Being filled with the fruits of righteousness, which are by Jesus Christ unto the glory and praise of God" (Phil 1:9-11). But a short prayer, you see, and yet full of good desires for the church, from the beginning to the end; that it may stand and go on, and that in the most excellent frame of spirit, even without blame, sincere, and without offence, until the day of Christ, let its temptations or persecutions be what they will (Eph 1:16-21; 3:14-19; Col 1:9-13).

Seventh. And because, as I said, prayer doth SUBMIT TO THE WILL OF GOD, and say, Thy will be done, as Christ hath taught us (Matt 6:10); therefore the people of the Lord in humility are to lay themselves and their prayers, and all that they have, at the foot of their God, to be disposed of by him as he in his heavenly wisdom seeth best. Yet not doubting but God will answer the desire of his people that way that shall be most for their advantage and his glory. When the saints therefore do pray with submission to the will of God, it doth not argue that they are to doubt or question God's love and kindness to them. But because they at all times are not so wise, but that sometimes Satan may get that advantage of them, as to tempt them to pray for that which, if they had it, would neither prove to God's glory nor his people's good. "Yet this is the confidence that we have in him, that if we ask anything according to his will, he heareth us; and if we know that he hear us, whatsoever we ask, we know that we have the petitions that we desired of him," that is, we asking in the Spirit of grace and supplication (I John 5:14,15). For, as I said before, that petition that is not put up in and through the Spirit, it is not to be answered, because it is beside the will of God. For the Spirit only knoweth that, and so consequently knoweth how to pray according to that will of God. "For what man knoweth the things of a man, save the spirit of man which is in him? even so the things of God knoweth no man but the Spirit of God" (I Cor 2:11). But more of this hereafter. Thus you see, first, what prayer is. Now to proceed.

[WHAT IT IS TO PRAY WITH THE SPIRIT.]

SECOND. I will pray with the Spirit. Now to pray with the Spirit--for that is the praying man, and none else, so as to be accepted of God--it is for a man, as aforesaid, sincerely and sensibly, with affection, to come to God through Christ, &c.; which sincere, sensible, and affectionate coming must be by the working of God's Spirit.

There is no man nor church in the world that can come to God in prayer, but by the assistance of the Holy Spirit. "For through Christ we all have access by one Spirit unto the Father" (Eph 2:18). Wherefore Paul saith, "For we know not what we should pray for as we ought; but the Spirit itself maketh intercession for us with groanings which cannot be uttered. And he that searcheth the hearts, knoweth what is the mind of the Spirit, because he maketh intercession for the saints according to the will of God" (Rom 8:26,27). And because there is in this scripture so full a discovery of the spirit of prayer, and of man's inability to pray without it; therefore I shall in a few words comment upon it.

"For we." Consider first the person speaking, even Paul, and, in his person, all the apostles. We apostles, we extraordinary officers, the wise master-builders, that have some of us been caught up into paradise (Rom 15:16; I Cor 3:10; II Cor 12:4). "We know not what we should pray for." Surely there is no man but will confess, that Paul and his companions were as able to have done any work for God, as any pope or proud prelate in the church of Rome, and could as well have made a Common Prayer Book as those who at first composed this; as being not a whit behind them either in grace or gifts.9

"For we know not what we should pray for." We know not the matter of the things for which we should pray, neither the object to whom we pray, nor the medium by or through whom we pray; none of these things know we, but by the help and assistance of the Spirit. Should we pray for communion with God through Christ? should we pray for faith, for justification by grace, and a truly sanctified heart? none of these things know we. "For what man knoweth the things of a man, save the spirit of man which is in him? even so the things of God knoweth no man, but the Spirit of God" (I Cor 2:11). But here, alas! the apostles speak of inward and spiritual things, which the world knows not (Isa 29:11).

Again, as they know not the matter, &c., of prayer, without the help of the Spirit; so neither know they the manner thereof without the same; and therefore he adds, "We know not what we should pray for as we ought"; but the Spirit helpeth our infirmities, with sighs and groans which cannot be uttered. Mark here, they could not so well and so fully come off in the manner of performing this duty, as these in our days think they can.

The apostles, when they were at the best, yea, when the Holy Ghost assisted them, yet then they were fain to come off with sighs and groans, falling short of expressing their mind, but with sighs and groans which cannot be uttered.

But here now, the wise men of our days are so well skilled as that they have both the manner and matter of their prayers at their finger-ends; setting such a prayer for such a day, and that twenty years before it comes. One for Christmas, another for Easter, and six days after that. They have also bounded how many syllables must be said in every one of them at their public exercises. For each saint's day, also, they have them ready for the generations yet unborn to say. They can tell you, also, when you shall kneel, when you shall stand, when you should abide in your seats, when you should go up into the chancel, and what you should do when you come there. All which the apostles came short of, as not being able to compose so profound a manner; and that for this reason included in this scripture, because the fear of God tied them to pray as they ought.

"For we know not what we should pray for as we ought." Mark this, "as we ought." For the not thinking of this word, or at least the not understanding it in the spirit and truth of it, hath occasioned these men to devise, as Jeroboam did, another way of worship, both for matter and manner, than is revealed in the Word of God (I Kings 12:26-33). But, saith Paul, we must pray as we ought; and this WE cannot do by all the art, skill, and cunning device of men or angels. "For we know not what we should pray for as we ought, but the Spirit"; nay, further, it must be "the Spirit ITSELF" that helpeth our infirmities; not the Spirit and man's lusts; what man of his own brain may imagine and devise, is one thing, and what they are commanded, and ought to do, is another. Many ask and have not, because they ask amiss; and so are never the nearer the enjoying of those things they petition for (James 4:3). It is not to pray at random that will put off God, or cause him to answer. While prayer is making, God is searching the heart, to see from what root and spirit it doth arise (I John 5:14). "And he that searcheth the heart knoweth," that is, approveth only, the meaning "of the Spirit, because he maketh intercession for the saints according to the will of God." For in that which is according to his will only, he heareth us, and in nothing else. And it is the Spirit only that can teach us so to ask; it only being able to search out all things, even the deep things of God. Without which Spirit, though we had a thousand Common Prayer Books, yet we know not what we should pray for as we ought, being accompanied with those infirmities that make us absolutely incapable of such a work. Which infirmities, although it is a hard thing to name them all, yet some of them are these that follow.

First. Without the Spirit man is so infirm that he cannot, with all other means whatsoever, be enabled to think one right saving thought of God, of Christ, or of his blessed things; and therefore he saith of the wicked, "God is not in all his thoughts," (Psa 10:4); unless it be that they imagine him altogether such a one as themselves (Psa 50:21). For "every imagination of the thoughts of his heart was only evil," and that "continually" (Gen 6:5; 8:21).

They then not being able to conceive aright of God to whom they pray, of Christ through whom they pray, nor of the things for which they pray, as is before showed, how shall they be able to address themselves to God, without the Spirit help this infirmity? Peradventure you will say, By the help of the Common Prayer Book; but that cannot do it, unless it can open the eyes, and reveal to the soul all these things before touched. Which that it cannot, it is evident; because that is the work of the Spirit only. The Spirit itself is the revealer of these things to poor souls, and that which doth give us to understand them; wherefore Christ tells his disciples, when he promised to send the Spirit, the Comforter, "He shall take of mine and show unto you"; as if he had said, I know you are naturally dark and ignorant as to the understanding any of my things; though ye try this course and the other, yet your ignorance will still remain, the veil is spread over your heart, and there is none can take away the same, nor give you spiritual understanding but the Spirit. The Common Prayer Book will not do it, neither can any man expect that it should be instrumental that way, it being none of God's ordinances; but a thing since the Scriptures were written, patched together one piece at one time, and another at another; a mere human invention and institution, which God is so far from owning of, that he expressly forbids it, with any other such like, and that by manifold sayings in his most holy and blessed Word. (See Mark 7:7,8, and Col 2:16-23; Deut 12:30-32; Prov 30:6; Deut 4:2; Rev 22:18). For right prayer must, as well in the outward part of it, in the outward expression, as in the inward intention, come from what the soul doth apprehend in the light of the Spirit; otherwise it is condemned as vain and an abomination, because the heart and tongue do not go along jointly in the same, neither indeed can they, unless the Spirit help our infirmities (Mark 7; Prov 28:9; Isa 29:13). And this David knew full well, which did make him cry, "Lord, open thou my lips, and my mouth shall show forth thy praise" (Psa 51:15). I suppose there is none can imagine but that David could speak and express himself as well as others, nay, as any in our generation, as is clearly manifested by his word and his works. Nevertheless when this good man, this prophet, comes into God's worship, then the Lord must help, or he can do nothing. "Lord, open thou my lips, and" then "my mouth shall show forth thy praise." He could not speak one right word, except the Spirit itself gave utterance. "For we know not what we should pray for as we ought, but the Spirit itself helpeth our infirmities." But,

Second. It must be a praying with the Spirit, that is, the effectuarical costumes of the last half century, but a few of the most effective floral costumes will be appended for the benefit of those who desire to introduce them into various entertainments.

The steady patronage of Her Majesty the Queen and the Royal Family have done much to remove any prejudices which existed against the drama, and as a powerful auxiliary to education the stage is rapidly gaining ground. Dull, indeed, must the theatre-goer be if he leaves without having assimilated some valuable lesson. To Shakespeare we owe many ideal types of womanhood, all the more precious now that some of the weaker sex, in an insatiable desire for progress, sometimes neglect those lesser arts which in the past proved to them a shield and buckler. The classical and historical pieces allow us to live again in scenes which occurred when the world was young, and convince us, though the tastes of the people were simpler, human nature, with its passions and aspirations, has changed but little. Who can deny the moral influence of such plays as "The Sign of the Cross," "Hypatia," "The Daughters of Babylon," "Virginius," or those of the Robertson school, of which "Caste" and "Ours" are examples? A love of music is not considered a marked trait of the English nation, yet have not Italian and comic opera stimulated a desire for a concord of sweet sounds among all classes of the community? Such plays as "Patience" and the "Mikado" have developed our instinct for colour and form, and we are taught the value of industry and restraint when we watch well-trained actors, capable of controlling every gesture, and of charming us with their well-modulated voices. Our lives are cheered by viewing the comic side of things, and on our clothing and household possessions, the stage has also laid a refining hand.

FLORAL COSTUMES.

A POPPY.

The bodice and skirt of red accordion, pleated mousseline de soie, the petals of the flower and belt in bright red silk. Large silk poppies appear on the shoulders and bust, and one of extra size is used for a head-dress. With this costume neat black shoes and silk stockings should be worn, and a palm-leaf fan covered with poppies and foliage should be carried.

LILY OF THE VALLEY.

Corsage and skirt of white pleated Valenciennes lace mounted on green silk. A full berthe of the flowers. White lace hat entirely covered with these blooms, and fan to correspond.

MOSS ROSE.

Gown of pink satin, veiled with tulle and flecked with rose buds. A ruche of moss roses at the hem of the skirt and on the bodice. A Dolly Varden hat trimmed with moss roses and pink ribbon.

WILD ROSE.

Dress of shot pink and white satin, embroidered or painted with clusters and trails of wild roses and foliage. Skirt edged with full ruche of pink tulle studded with roses, and corsage trimmed to correspond. Coiffure poudr?dressed with small basket of roses and pink ribbon.

WHITE ROSE.

Gown with Watteau train of white satin edged with leaveless roses, chains of the same flowers carried across the front of the dress, and outlining the square-cut bodice, and elbow sleeves. Ruffles of lace. A wreath of white roses in the powdered hair, and a crook decorated with flowers and ribbon streamers.

SUMMER ROSES.

Gown of cream-coloured brocade, with design in shaded roses and foliage, trimmed with garland of roses of different tints embedded in tulle. Corsage trimmed to correspond, and a damask rose worn in the hair.

WILD FLOWERS.

Dress of pale blue satin, veiled with green tulle. Trails of forget-me-nots, poppies, marguerites, buttercups, and grass depending from the waist-belt to edge of skirt, and bodice trimmed to correspond. A Leghorn hat garnished with wild flowers, grass, and blue ribbons.

GARDENIA.

Greek dress of white cr 正 e de Chine, embroidered in classical design with silver. In front diagonal trails of gardenias and their dark foliage arranged from the right shoulder to left side of dress. The hair bound with silver bands. A shower bouquet to correspond.

THE SHAMROCK.

Gown of emerald green satin applique with velvet shamrocks of a darker shade. The stomacher a large trefoil in emeralds, and the short sleeves cut to resemble the Irish emblem. Corsage veiled with green tulle strewn with tiny shamrocks, and a coronet of the same in the hair.

THE THISTLE.

High dress of eau de nil satin. The skirt edged with a wreath of thistles, which are also embroidered in a bold design on the front of gown and bodice. Satin hat trimmed with thistles and ribbon, and black staff tied with thistles and ribbon streamers.

DANDELION.

Gown of yellow accordion, pleated chiffon finished on the skirt with trails of flowers from the waist to hem of the skirt, interspersed with the seed pods commonly known as blow-aways. The bodice of pleated yellow chiffon with dandelions across the berthe and clusters on the shoulders. A wreath and aigrette to correspond.

IRIS.

Dress of white satin, veiled with mauve chiffon, flecked with iris petals. Trails of mauve and white flowers tied with bows of satin in alternate shades, and carried across the skirt. Square cut corsage to correspond, and elbow sleeves. A muslin cap trimmed with the same flowers. Powdered hair.

LILAC.

Gown of cream satin brocaded with mauve and white lilac, Marie Antoinette, white chiffon fichu, and cap trimmed with clusters of shaded lilac and foliage. Elbow sleeves with chiffon ruffles. The white satin fan painted to correspond, and caught by a flower chatelaine. The hair dressed with the same flowers, and a twisted scarf of mauve and white chiffon.

www.ingramcontent.com/pod-product-compliance
Lightning Source LLC
Chambersburg PA
CBHW070915180526
45168CB00005B/2026